READING PAULO FREIRE

SUNY SERIES, TEACHER EMPOWERMENT
AND SCHOOL REFORM

HENRY A. GIROUX AND PETER L. MCLAREN, EDITORS

Reading Paulo Freire

His Life and Work

Moacir Gadotti

Translated by John Milton

State University of New York Press

Published by
State University of New York Press, Albany

For information, address State University of New York Press,
State University Plaza, Albany, N.Y. 12246

Production by M.R. Mulholland
Marketing by Dana E. Yanulavich

Library of Congress Cataloging-in-Publication Data

Gadotti, Moacir.
    Reading Paulo Freire : his life and work / Moacir Gadotti :
translated by John Milton.
        p. cm. — (SUNY series, teacher empowerment and school
reform)
    Includes bibliographical references (p.   ).
    ISBN 0-7914-1923-1. — ISBN 0-7914-1924-X (pbk.)
    1. Freire, Paulo, 1921-   . 2. Educators—Brazil—Biography.
3. Educaton—Philosophy. 4. Popular education. 5. Critical
pedagogy.   I. Title. II. Series: Teacher empowerment and
school reform.
LB880.F732G34 1994
370'.1—dc20   93-26751
                                                              CIP

10 9 8 7 6 5 4 3 2 1

Contents

Foreword:
A Land of Contrasts and
a Pedagogy of Contradiction

Brazil is a land of contrasts. Land of wonderful Rio de Janeiro, with the beautiful sights of the Corcovado mountain and its splendid world-class beaches, but also land of the Amazonian Indians, harased, haunted, and murdered in their own dominion by gold prospectors and entrepreneurs of many sorts. Brazil is the land of joy expressed in the Brazilian music like *samba* or *lambada*, and the skillful soccer that is played in beaches, parks, and everywhere, but it is also the land of sorrow, ever-present in the widespread urban violence in Rio de Janeiro and every major urban center; in the killing of *meninos da rua*, the children living in the streets; in the growing numbers of the rural and urban poor that make up one-fifth of the Brazilian population. It is this Brazil that with a GNP of $375 billion in 1991 ranked tenth among hte industrial powers in the world system, this Brazil that is dressed both in the glamor of its riches and the bitter *saveur* of poverty, that this book about Paulo Freire is situated in, narrated as a personal experience by Moacir Gadotti, professor of the University of São Paulo.

Moacir Gadotti was born half a century ago in Santa Catarina, in southern Brazil. The middle son of a family of Italian poor peasants, he grew up among ten siblings speaking Italian until he entered elementary school, where he learned the national language, Portuguese. It seems that his appetite for languages did not stop there because he studied also French, Spanish, English, German, Latin, and Greek. He obtained a B.A. and M.A. in Philosophy in Brazil, and his Ph.D. in Education at the University of Geneva (Switzerland) in 1977. Like many Brazilian intellectuals, Gadotti returned to Brazil in 1977 to confront the rampant authoritarianism of the military government that took power in 1964 and sent to exile many Brazilian intellectuals, Paulo Freire included.

The struggle against authoritarianism in Brazil, and the exploration of the work of Paulo Freire, whom he had met in Geneva in the early seventies, marked the beginnings of Moacir Gadotti's academic career. Like many Brazilian professors returning to Brazil, Gadotti had to accept two university positions to survive. He worked as a Professor of Philosophy of Education at the Catholic University of São Paulo, and at the University of Campinas (UNICAMP, one of the premier research universities in the country), a hundred kilometers away.

For a philosopher of education deeply concerned with the notion of contradiction, resistance, and praxis of liberation, this geographical location couldn't have been more appropriate for his work. The State of São Paulo was the center of the opposition to the military government. The strikes by metalworkers of São Bernardo—an industrial region of São Paulo—in 1978 and 1979 sparked strikes all over Brazil, with more than three million workers defying state authoritarianism. In 1979, in diverse meetings celebrated throughout the country, more than one hundred people, including members of Congress, union leaders, and intellectuals, Moacir Gadotti among them, decided to launch the *Partido dos Trabalhadores*, Workers' Party, or PT, a socialist democratic party.

In the acts of creation of the party on February 10, 1980, Moacir Gadotti signed in representation of Paulo Freire who, from Geneva, had enthusiastically adhered to the newly created mass party. Between 1980 and 1982 the PT grew from a few thousand to 212,000 members, being officially granted its provisional registration as a national political party on February 11, 1982.[1]

The PT has been playing a forceful role in the process of democratization of Brazil. Its leader, metalworker Luis Inácio Lula da Silva (*Lula*), was the runner-up in the 1989 presidential campaign that elected Collor, the first president ever impeached by Congress in Brazil. Today, Lula is ranked by political pools as a serious candidate in the next presidential elections of 1994, quite a remarkable situation for a leftist candidate in the landscape of neoliberal governments in Latin America.

For many years, Moacir Gadotti chaired the Educational Commission of the PT in São Paulo, helping to devise a socialist democratic educational policy for Brazil. When the PT won the 1989 municipal elections in São Paulo, Gadotti joined Paulo Freire, who was appointed Secretary of Education of the Municipality of São Paulo by Mayor Luiza Erundina, becoming Freire's Chief of Cabinet until Freire resigned to continue with his writing and lecturing in 1991.

Moacir Gadotti has developed an original approach to the notion of *popular public school* which links closely the key demands of a socialist democratic approach to schooling (school autonomy, quality of education) with the tradition of free, mandatory, and compulsory public schooling in Latin America.[2] Gadotti's view, while not exactly the same, is very close to the positions that Paulo Freire has defended for more than four decades. Not only is there a compatibility of theoretical and political views, and a long friendship between Gadotti and Freire, but Moacir Gadotti was also very instrumental in helping Freire to secure a university teaching position when he returned to Brazil in 1980 from his exile in Geneva, despite the myriad of obstacles put forward by conservatives in academia and government.

Drawing from his work and his association with Freire that has spanned two decades, Moacir Gadotti offers in this book a fresh political view and a biographical analysis of Freire's life and work. Written in jargon-free, straightforward manner for elementary and secondary school teachers, this book is rich in biographical and firsthand accounts, and provides graphic images of Freire's work in Brazil and elsewhere, offering also documented accounts of sources that influenced Freire, and interpretations about the political philosophy of the creator of *Pedagogy of the Oppressed*.

Brazil, a land of contrast, displays in a Hegelian fashion the contradiction between universality and particularity—a feature well captured by Moacir Gadotti in discussing the dialectical tensions between Freire's original proposals in northeast Brazil, and the reverberation of his work worldwide. The quality of descriptions and analysis, and the tension between particularity and universality makes this book about Paulo Freire particularly intriguing and appealing for the English reader in our incomplete modernity.

Carlos Alberto Torres
Agoura, California, September 1993

Foreword

Few educators have received as much widespread acclaim and worldwide recognition as the Brazilian educator Paulo Freire. His singular contribution to the development of critical social theory and his personal involvement in literacy campaigns, educational movements, and an astonishing array of political and educational projects has revolutionized on an international scale the meaning of pedagogy and its relationship to the making of both personal and collective history.

Freire's presence on the world stage as a "man of his time" has provided the conditions for countless individuals, regardless of race, gender, class, and caste, to break free from their historically contingent and entrenched vocabularies to face up to their fallibility and strength as agents of possibility. As the standard-bearer of what has come to be known as critical pedagogy, Freire continues to identify and challenge not only those pedagogical mechanisms central to the phenomenon of oppression but also those relations within wider social, cultural, and institutional contexts that confront individuals with the logic of domination in the guise of grand narratives of reason and univocal meaning in the service of capital.

Rather than ground his pedagogy in a doctrinal absolutism, Freire's attention is always fixed on important social issues. What has endeared several generations of critical educators to Freire, both in terms of a respect for his political vision and for the way he conducts his own life, is the manner in which he has situated his work within an ethics of pragmatism, love, and solidarity.

Moacir Gadotti's book, *Reading Paulo Freire: His Life and Work* is more than a monument to Freire's continuing contribution to a praxis of liberation; it is a sensitive interpretation of and personal commentary on the relationship of Freire's philosophy of liberation to the central historical events that have shaped Freire's life. Recognized as one of the foremost authorities on Freire's work, as well as a distinguished educational theorist in his own right, Gadotti offers us an intimate and compassionate—but not uncritical—treatment of Freire's central ideas and achievements.

Gadotti situates Freire, first and foremost, as a "militant educator," a revolutionary who has "tried not to dichotomize his task with the liberation of the oppressed." Through vivid and often poignant anecdotal accounts, Gadotti traverses with keen insight Freire's tumultuous history, from his condemnation, imprisonment and exile by the leaders of Brazil's 1964 military coup, who accused Freire of being an "international subversive" and a "traitor of Christ and the Brazilian people" and denounced his writing as comparable "to that of Stalin, Hitler, Peron, and Mussolini," to Freire's ten years of international service with the World Council of Churches, to his eventual return to Brazil in March, 1980, and his subsequent work as Secretary of Education of São Paulo and his inauguration of MOVA-SP (Literacy Movement in the city of São Paulo), which is based on Freire's work and that of Pedro Pontual and continues up to the present day.

Gadotti reflects upon the development of the central concepts and themes that drive Freire's work, from his conception of dialogue (which Gadotti describes as "a horizontal relationship. . . fed by love, humility, hope, faith and confidence") to his ideas of coherence, democratic radicalism, recovering citizenship, and interdisciplinarity, to name just a few. Throughout Gadotti's discussion of Freire's work, whether related to Freire's early anti-colonialist struggles with Amílcar Cabral's PAIGC in Guinea-Bissau, the MPLA of Angola, or FRELIMO in Mozambique, or his contribution to Partido dos Trabalhadores, in his native Brazil, we rarely lose sight of the intensely intimate connection between Freire's own praxis of the possible and the ongoing development of Freire's thought.

Reading Paulo Freire underscores a number of important conceptual themes that undoubtedly will prove valuable to North American educational and cultural workers largely unfamililar with Freire's work. One is the manner in which knowledge is emphasized as an "act of knowing" that is deeply inscribed in pedagogical, cultural, and institutional practices. Another is the process by which, in Freirean praxis, the realms of the ethical and rational become dialectically re-initiating and mutually constitutive. Equally edifying is Freire's conceptual understanding of how the power of institu-tionalized schooling finds its correlative in particular regimes of knowledge that stress technocratic reasoning and an introduction to a model of citizenship based on an individualist and consumerist ethics. One of the great strengths of Freire's work, as Gadotti is quick to recognize, is his recognition of the ways in which power is subjacent to systems of intelligibility, social formations, and the role of the state. Resisting the aestheticization of politics (which Walter Benjamin, it may be noted, concluded to be the ineluctable mark of fascism), Freire has also consistently attacked forms of pedagogy that attribute great hermeneutical power to the figure of the master, prefering instead to situate teaching in the performative mode of dialogue. Teaching for Freire is not an exegetical practice reserved only for experts or educational specialists but is located in the historically open ability of individuals to learn from their own experiences by developing a language of analysis that challenges the formation of their lives as they have been constructed from within hegemonic relations of domination and subordination, power and privilege, affirmation and negation, and caught within the tension between a resignation to despair and a loyalty and commitment to hope. Above all, Gadotti captures, often with poignant directness, Freire's affirmation of the radicalization of the revolutionary against the sectarianism of the reactionary, and the militancy of the spirit against the political quietism of the custodians of tradition.

In the final sections of *Reading Paulo Freire*, Freire's work is read presciently against the contributions of Carl Rogers, Ivan Illich, John Dewey, and Lev Vygotsky. The book succeeds in removing the life and work of Paulo Freire out of the narrow context of "popular adult literacy schemes" in order to situate it in a much broader and deeper view of education and cultural politics. A closing epilogue takes the form of a dialogue between Freire and Gadotti and manages to reverently capture in a manner admirably devoid of sentimentality and apocalyptic overtones, the spirit of the mature Freire, now in his seventies. Here we encounter Freire in his own words as a proud yet eminently humble warrior of the spirit who describes his present contribution to education as engaging in "a bohemian pedagogy of happiness"—a pedagogy that he elaborates with both the wisdom of an ancient sage and the unfailing passion of the socialist revolutionary as "a pedagogy of laughter, of questioning, of curiosity, of seeing the future through the present, a pedagogy that believes in the possibility of the transformation of the world, that believes in history as a possibility."

Peter L. McLaren
Henry A. Giroux

Introduction

This book, an introduction to the work of Paulo Freire, is aimed mainly at readers who are unfamiliar with his work, educators, and people interested in education. I begin by outlining the development of his ideas on education and then relate them to the historical context and to Freire's life.

Writing a book with these characteristics is a considerable challenge. Firstly, there is the challenge of the scope of the work of Paulo Freire. It has a strong historical basis and contains hundreds of speeches, papers, conversations, and interviews. Any attempt to cover everything that has been said, written, or recorded would be totally impossible. All that we can do is to underline his position and the philosophy of education which runs through his struggle and his historicocultural legacy.

I have attempted to write a book on education as Paulo Freire himself would have done, using a method and learning through victories and defeats in the same way one learns in life. I have tried to follow a chronological line in which life and work are naturally mixed. In many cases I have let Paulo Freire's work speak for itself.

This book involved the study of a large number of letters. As documents they are very interesting, and through them we can see Paulo Freire's personality. They were written by people with whom he had close contact and who learned from his presence, his attention, and the seriousness with which he treated every communication. Let us look at two examples.

On September 19th, 1983, his birthday, he received a letter from twenty-four public schoolchildren in São Pedro, São Paulo state, who asked him to "continue loving children for ever."

On September 28 Paulo Freire replied to the letter:

> Dear Friends from the First Grade at Gustavo Teixeira School,
>
> I received your letter today at the University of Campinas. I was very happy to see you had such a lot of confidence in me when you asked me to continue loving children. I was also very pleased by the coincidence that you wrote to me on my birthday. On this day my seven grandchildren came to have dinner at my house, and they gave me presents that they themselves had chosen, and then they played with me.
>
> I promise I will never stop loving children. I love life too much.
>
> > With love from
> > Paulo Freire

There are many such examples of affection, recognition of his work, and photos of helpers. The chance of examining them was a rich and gratifying experience and allowed me to write this book with enormous enthusiasm.

When I was organizing the book, I was thinking that it would be read by high school pupils, the teachers of the future, who would initially be full of love and hope for their chosen profession—dealing with children—and who, after a number of years in the teaching profession, with its low salaries and poor working conditions, might lose all

FIGURE 1

This Photo was sent to Paulo Freire in 1986 by one of his readers, an educator who applied his ideas in approximately 80 classes with the nomads people of the desert of Kenya.

enthusiasm. I hope that this book can show them the example of a life which has been devoted to education in adverse conditions, but which has been able to take advantage of these adversities and limitations and which has been able to learn from them and with them.

The reader should not look in the book for magic formulas from which he or she will be able to mechanically extract better results for his or her own teaching. However, I haven't entirely left aside an analysis of the concrete proposals which are an integral part of the philosophy of Paulo Freire. His enormous experience and his theories, which have been the result of working in various parts of the world, will certainly help us to understand our own very different contexts and will help us to teach more efficiently and objectively.

The importance of Paulo Freire's ideas does not come just from their universal value, but also from the fact that the world situation today is not very different from that in which Paulo Freire developed his ideas.

Recovering the meaning and importance of teaching as part of the civilizing process is quite definitely one of the main challenges that today's young educators will face. The life and work of an optimistic educator like Paulo Freire should act as a stimulus for us to continue the collective task of social reconstruction. In this task the educator has considerable influence and, in the long run, a central role.

Let us now look at some commentaries on Paulo Freire and his work.

Linda Bimbi, referring to the impossibility of classifying Paulo Freire in any school of educators, in the preface to the Italian edition of *Pedagogy of the Oppressed*, writes: "The impossibility of classifying him comes from his absolute incompatibility with schemes, which is the visceral expression of his connection with the land and with mankind. He thus represents the authentic intellectual in our world, who comes from the peoples who are emerging nowadays to be part of history."[1] He is seen as a new kind of intellectual, "organic," in the words of Gramsci.[2]

The well-known philosopher and writer, Roger Garaudy, quotes the work of Paulo Freire as an example of the struggle for the construction of a socialist society with a "human face" and as an example of the importance of the countries of the Third World in social and educational questions. He finds the fact that "the greatest educator of our time" is Brazilian is important, due to the fact that Paulo Freire gave literacy and education in general the mission of awakening in people a critical and militant conscience, a "pedagogy of the oppressed," and a "practice of freedom."[3]

In August 1986, the *New York Times* published an article which stressed the importance of Paulo Freire in the organization of various educational systems.[4]

He was called "the greatest specialist in literacy movements and radical educator in the world," "radical" meaning here "left-wing." In the United States, Paulo Freire's ideas have been adopted by feminists, blacks, and Hispanics in teacher-training programs and in other areas such as health, economics, and sociology.

His educational ideas have, however, met with resistance from the dominant classes in his own country although they have spread through all of Latin America, Africa, and the highly developed countries.

But who is this educator called Paulo Freire?

1

We Can Also Learn in the Shade of the Mangoes

Son of Joaquim Temistocles Freire, an army sergeant from Rio Grande do Norte and of Edeltrudes Neves Freire, a housewife and seamstress from Pernambuco (Brazil), Paulo Reglus Neves Freire was born on September 19th, 1921 in Recife, in the district of Casa Amarela, at number 724 on the road to Encanamento. His father was responsible for his name. It should have been Re-gu-lus, but a mistake was made at the Registry Office. In his teens he began to be called just Paulo Freire.

His mother was ten years younger than his father. A spiritualist, she had completed high school and spoke French well. Both parents were strongly marked by the patriachal and macho culture of the Northeast of Brazil at the beginning of the century. Paulo was the youngest of four children, of whom two died without his having known them. The first stages of his education were somewhat strict. "My father," he said later, "always lived at the midpoint between the opposite poles of freedom and authority. He was an army officer, but not an authoritarian. This was very different to my mother's way of being. She was very quiet and soft, much more so than he. He was also very affectionate, but he was less tender than my mother."[1]

Paulo learned to read with his parents, in the shade of the trees in the yard of the house in which he was born. This experience came through his own words, words from his infancy and childhood, not from the experience of his parents. This fact would influence his work, years later. His chalk was the twigs of the mango tree in whose shade he learned to read, and his blackboard was the ground. This formation and information was all given informally, before school. It was a living, free, unpretentious preschool.

His first school actually was a small private school belonging to a teacher who died in 1978. He went there already knowing his alphabet, writing well and copying. He studied there for little over a year but would never forget something which was called "making sentences." It was an exercise which he liked a lot: the teacher asked him to write two or three words and then asked him to say something with those words. She had a very definite oral intuition of the necessity of the child to exercise his expressivity. If he made a mistake when he wrote, he would be corrected during and after. There were no abstractions.

At this school, Paulo Freire was introduced to verbs. But, instead of memorizing the present indicative tense of the verb *to have*, he lived the verb *to have* in the indicative present as he lived it in the past tense. After all, verbs are learned like this, and not in the way that many people teach them, through mechanical memorization. The "I am" in itself, in the pure recitation of the verb tense, has no meaning at all.

A Teenager Who Considered Himself Ugly

Paulo Freire had a happy childhood, but at a very early age, like the majority of Brazilians from the

Northeast, he knew the meaning of hunger and misery. He was eight when the effects of the world economic crisis of 1929 were felt in the Northeast of Brazil. In 1931 the crisis made the Freire family move to Jaboatão, twelve miles from Recife, where survival seemed less difficult. Paulo was thirteen when his father died. These problems meant that his studies had to be put off. He only entered the *ginásio* (high school), now the fifth series of the first grade, when he was sixteen. All his classmates were eleven or twelve.

Paulo Freire recounts that almost all his classmates were well-dressed, well-fed, and came from homes which had a certain culture. "I was tall, lanky, wore pants which were too short and risked being made fun of because of their length. They were shorter than the length of my legs."[2] He admits that he had the feeling that he was an ugly teenager. He rejected his own body, which was too bony. He was afraid of asking questions in class because, as he was older than his classmates, he felt obliged to ask questions that were more intelligent and pertinent than the rest of the class.

But living in Jaboatão, playing knockabout games of soccer, he also had contact with children and teenagers from poor rural families and the children of workers who lived in the hills or near the canals. "My experience with them," says Paulo Freire, "helped me to get used to a different way of thinking and expressing myself. This was the grammar of the people, the language of the people, and as an educator of the people I devote myself today to the rigorous understanding of this language."[3]

Paulo Freire always had great difficulty in assimilating any kind of formal education. But he began to teach at a very early age, when he was still a high school student. He remembers that he had written, three years earlier, the word *rato* (mouse) with two r's.

His mother brought him up in the Catholic religion, and this would also be an important influence both on his pedagogical theories and on his practice—he was a militant in the Catholic Action movement.[4] Freire never denied his Christian upbringing; in fact, he has always considered Christianity progressive. But he would criticize what he called the church of the oppressors, opposing it to the prophetic church, the church of the oppressed: "The prophetic church is the church of hope, hope which only exists in the future, a future which only the oppressed classes have, as the future of the dominant classes is a pure repetition of their present state of being the oppressors."[5]

He frequently wrote to his mother, who died in 1978, when he was still in exile.

He was over twenty when he obtained a place in the Faculty of Law of Recife. Then he met Elza Maia Costa de Oliveira, a primary school teacher who taught children how to read and write. She was five years older than he. They got married in 1944 when Freire was twenty-three and was working as a secondary schoolteacher. It was Elza who stimulated him to systematically devote himself to his studies, and she even helped him to elaborate the method which has made him so well-known.

Paulo Freire always refers to Elza with considerable affection: "My meeting her was one of the most creative meetings in my life," he once said. They had five children: Maria Madalena, Maria Cristina, Maria de Fátima, Joaquim, and Lutgardes. The three daughters followed the footsteps of their father and became educators. Paulo Freire continues: "Elza was marvelous and continues to be. She is a permanent presence and stimulation in my life. For example, when I was in prison in 1964, Elza visited me and brought me pans full of food for all my cellmates. She never told me, 'Look, if you had thought a little more . . . if you had avoided certain things, you wouldn't be here.' Never. Her solidarity was total and still is."[6]

Paulo Freire lost Elza on October 24, 1986 after forty years of "being sweethearts."[7]

Teaching as a Passion

I wanted very much to study, but I couldn't as our economic condition didn't allow me to. I tried to read or pay attention in the classroom, but I didn't understand anything because of my hunger. I wasn't dumb. It wasn't lack of interest. My social condition didn't allow me to have an education. Experience showed me once again the relationship between social class and knowledge. So, because of my problems, my older brother began to work and to help us, and I began to eat more. At that time, I was in the second or third year of high school, and I always had problems. When I began to eat better, I began understanding better what I was reading. It was just as this time that I began to study grammar as I loved language problems. I studied the philosophy of language on my own and got myself ready to understand structuralism and language when I was eighteen or nineteen. Then I began teaching Portuguese grammar with love for language and philosophy and with the intuition that I should understand the expectations of the pupils and make them participate in the dialogue. At a certain moment, between the ages of fifteen and twenty-three, I discovered that teaching was my passion."[8]

In 1946, living again in Recife, Paulo Freire began to work at SESI (Social Service of Industry), where he stayed eight years.

FIGURE 2

Paulo Freire in Recife, in the early fifties as director of the Education Department of SESI (Social Service of Industry).

SESI is an employers' institution whose objectives are to assist. It was set up, according to Paulo Freire "not to criticize the consciousness of the working class, but to confuse reality and to put obstacles in the way of the fact that the working class could achieve its own identity."[9] But it was here that the reality became clear. It was here that Paulo Freire learned to talk with the working class and to understand their way of learning about the world through their language. And it was here that he became an educator, learning through his practice something that would always remain with him: *always think about the practice.*

Paulo Freire became educational director of SESI and coordinated the work of the teachers with the children, as well as working with their families. In these contacts between school and families, he learned that discussions of abstract concepts, for example the ethical code of the child in Piaget,[10] would not be able to sensitivize a concrete father, who hits a real child in a concrete situation. What would help was a discussion of the difficulties of someone who had too little to live on.

At SESI Paulo Freire was in charge of studying the relationships between pupils, teachers, and parents. And it was here that he discovered the roots of his anti-elitist and anti-idealistic pedagogy. He noticed the "idealistic" elements in the orientation given to working-class families, and the resulting mistakes, made him follow new directions. Paulo Freire attributed their problems to the difference between middle-class language and the popular language of the workers. Thus, a study of the language of the people was the starting point for the development of his work on popular education and his pedagogy.

Important experiences in his life at this time were his participation in the MCP (*Movement for Popular Culture*) of Recife[11] and the studies on popular and erudite language which he made as a teacher of Portuguese.

He read important Brazilian authors such as José Lins do Rego, Graciliano Ramos, Jorge Amado, Gilberto Freyre:

> I read them a lot. And they also remade me as a young teacher of grammar due to the aesthetic creativity of their language. Today I remember how I changed my teaching of syntax when I was about twenty. The important thing was, at that time, not just to deny the rules. When I was young, I learned that beauty and creativity couldn't be slaves of grammatical correctness. This taught me that creativity needed freedom. So, as a young teacher, I

changed my teaching and gave greater value to
creativity. This was also a basis for me to understand
later that creativity in teaching is linked to creativity
in politics. Authoritarian teaching, or an authoritarian political regime, doesn't allow the freedom
necessary for creativity. Creativity is necessary in
order to learn.[12]

Motivated by Elza, Paulo Freire devoted himself
entirely to educational work and abandoned his work as
a lawyer soon after his first case. Paulo Freire himself tells
the story: "I had to collect my fee. After talking to my
client, a young shy, frightened dentist, I decided not to
charge him. He was happy because I was this kind of
lawyer, and I was happy when I stopped being one."[13]

Paulo Freire was one of the founders of the Cultural
Extension Service of the University of Recife and was its
first director. From this experience he made his first
studies of a new method of teaching adult literacy, which
he demonstrated in 1958 at the Regional Preparatory
Seminar in Pernambuco under the title "Adult Education
and Marginal Populations: the Problem of the Mocambos
(slums in the Northeast of Brazil)."

In 1959 Paulo Freire wrote "Present-day Education
in Brazil," which was the thesis with which he competed
for the chair of History and Philosophy of Education in
the School of Fine Arts of Recife. This thesis gave him his
Ph.D.

In this thesis, the seeds of his theory and educational
practice can be found: "Paulo Freire criticizes Brazilian
school education and proposes a radical revision starting
from the study of the needs of the educational process in
particular historical circumstances. . . . The style, though
not forceful, does not hide Paulo Freire's acceptance of a

decisive point of view: all considerations of Brazilian school education cannot develop in the emptiness of abstract propositions."[14]

Paulo Freire's work at this time was clearly marked by nationalism and developmentalism. This was due to influence from authors connected to ISEB,[15] (Higher Institute for Brazilian Studies), who included Roland Corbisier, Álvaro Vieira Pinto, and Alberto Guerreiro Ramos.

Although Paulo Freire realizes that he made a number of errors and ingenuous proposals in this thesis, he was on the right track. As he would say later,[16] he defended "the exercise of democracy and talked about the importance of groups of ordinary people discussing their own street, their trade union, their children's school, the basic facilities of their district and even their own production. I don't regret saying in 1959 and I continue saying today, even with much more conviction, that the concrete elements of democracy must be lived without any fear in Brazil. And what must finish is this mania you find on the left of talking about democracy and being a social democrat."[17]

The following year, when he gave a lecture entitled "Primary Schooling for Brazil," he defended the idea that the problem of the primary school is not just that there are too few schools for the number of pupils but that the problem is equally their lack of "insertion" in the social context. Without this, schools give no hope and are "inadequate in relation to the great increase in democratization, closely connected to development, which is an integral part of the country." In a note he adds: "Even today I can't understand why no one has thought of offering the children of the Northeast of Brazil selections of 'popular ballads' in their reading books. These have both an aesthetic and a cultural value."[18]

In addition to the inadequacy of primary school, Paulo Freire draws attention to its *lack of organicity* in carrying out its specific functions:

> We can say that the type of school that we urgently need is a school in which you really study and work. When, together with other educators, we criticize the intellectualism of our school, we are not trying to defend a position for the school in which subjects and the discipline are diluted. In our history we have probably never had such a great necessity of teaching and of learning as today. Learning to read, write and tell. Studying history and geography. Understanding the situation and situations of the country. The intellectualism we are fighting against is just this hollow, empty, loud verbosity which has no relation to the surroundings in which we are born, we grow up in, and from which even today to a great extent, we are nurtured.[19]

At this time, Paulo Freire was making a proposal which only recently has been put into action: the setting up of parents' and pupils' associations and school councils with educational goals. These would associate the formation of a critical consciousness with popular organization.

The Act of Studying

Studying is, really, a difficult task. It demands a critical and systematic position. It demands an intellectual discipline which can only be gained in practice.

This is exactly what 'banking education'[20] fails to stimulate. On the contrary, its basis lies in killing curiosity, creativity, and any investigative spirit in the pupils. Its "discipline" is that of ingenuity before the text, in contrast to the critical element which should be necessary.

This ingenuous procedure to which the pupil is subjected may, in addition to other factors, be responsible for the way in which students whose reading becomes purely mechanical free themselves from the text and imagine themselves elsewhere. What they are asked to do is not to understand the content but to memorize it. If the student manages to do this, he will have answered the challenge.

In a more critical vision, things happen differently. The student of a text should feel challenged by the whole text and his or her objective should be to get hold of its deep meaning.

This fundamental, critical posture, an indispensable part of the act of studying, requires that whoever devotes themselves to it, takes on the role of the subject of the act.

This means that a serious study is impossible if the student of a text approaches it as if he were magnetized by the magical words of the author, behaving passively, "domestically," trying to do no more than memorize the statements of the author, letting himself be "occupied" by what the author states, being transformed into a container to be filled by the content of the text.

Seriously studying a text is to study the way in which the writer studied in order to write it. It means taking note of the *historicosociological conditioning of knowledge*. It means looking for relationships between the content under scrutiny and other connected areas of knowledge. Studying is a form of demanding, of recreating, of rewriting—a task for the subject and not for the object. Therefore, from this point of view, it is not possible for the student to get away from the text, to renounce a critical attitude toward it. . . .

It's no good jumping a page of a book if you haven't understood it. You must insist on unraveling it. Understanding of a text is not something that is given as a gift. It demands patient work from the reader who is puzzled.

Study can't be calculated from the number of pages read in a night or by the quantity of books read in the course of a semester.

Study is not an act of consuming ideas, but rather one of creating them and recreating them.[21]

The Act of Knowing

If we look at the cycle of discovery, we can see two moments, not more than two, that are dialectically related. The first moment of the cycle is the moment of production, production of a piece of knowledge, of something new. The other moment is when the piece of knowledge which has been produced is discovered or made known. One moment is the production of a piece of knowledge, and the second is when you discover something that already exists. What we generally do is that we dichotomize these two moments, isolating them from each other. As a consequence, we reduce the act of *discovering* existing knowledge to a mere *transference* of existing knowledge. And the teacher becomes the specialist in transferring knowledge. In this case, he loses some of the necessary and indispensable qualities which are required in the production of knowledge, as in the discovery of existing knowledge. Some of these qualities, for example, are action, critical reflection, curiosity, a demanding questioning, worry, uncertainty—all these virtues are indispensable for the subject who will understand! . . .

Another essential factor is that, when we separate the *production* of knowledge from the *discovery* of already existing knowledge, schools become easily transformed into shops for the sale of knowledge, which is part of capitalist ideology.[22]

2

The Method Which Took Paulo Freire into Exile

Paulo Freire's ideas of literacy and his theories of knowledge must be understood in their context: the circumstances of the Northeast of Brazil at the beginning of the sixties, where half of the inhabitants lived in the *culture of silence*—they were illiterate. It was necessary to "give them the word" so that they could "move" and could participate in the construction of a Brazil where they would be responsible for their own destiny and where colonialism would be overcome.[1]

The first experiments with the method began in the town of Angicos in the state of Rio Grande do Norte in 1962, where three hundred rural farm workers were taught how to read and write in forty-five days. The following year, Paulo Freire was invited by President João Goulart and by the Minister of Education, Paulo de Tarso Santos, to rethink the literacy schemes for adults on a national basis, in the same way Darcy Ribeiro had done with university reform and Lauro de Oliveira Lima had done with secondary schools. In 1964, twenty thousand cultural circles were programmed to be set up for two million illiterate people. The military coup, however, interrupted the work right at the beginning and canceled all the work that had already been done.

Paulo Freire presented his literacy method in more detailed form in 1967 in the book *Education as a Practice of Freedom*. This book was the result of the collective experience of more than fifteen years of work in adult literacy in both urban and rural proletarian and sub-proletarian areas and was helped enormously by the experience of Paulo Freire's sweetheart, wife, and companion, Elza.

Strictly speaking, one shouldn't speak about the Paulo Freire "method" as it is much more a theory of knowledge and an educational philosophy than a teaching method. However, Paulo Freire became well-known much more through the adult literacy scheme which takes his name. This method is called a system, philosophy, or theory of knowledge and the phases of development and uses of the method can be found in Paulo Freire's book *Conscientization*.

Linda Bimbi, in the preface to the Italian edition of *Pedagogy of the Oppressed*, said:

> The originality of Paulo Freire's method is not just in the efficiency of its literacy methods, but more especially in the novelty of its content to "con-scientize.". . .Conscientization comes from a certain educational context and has its own characteristics: (1) with the new techniques, a new vision of the world is learned, which contains a critique of present circumstances and a relative attempt to overcome these circumstances. The means for this quest are not imposed, but are left to the creative capacity of the "free" conscience; (2) A single isolated individual is not conscientized alone but as part of a community when it has total solidarity in relation to a common situation. However, the basis of the method, which

is that education is seen as a part of the global process of the revolutionary transformation of society, is a challenge to all prerevolutionary situations and suggests the creation of *humanizing*, not humanistic, educational acts, which would be incorporated in a pedagogy of revolution.[2]

Linda Bimbi thus attempts to demonstrate the clear connection between Paulo Freire's method and the movement for social transformation. This is the same as saying that Paulo Freire's method is linked to a total change in society.

Paulo Freire's literacy method grew from the MCP, the Movement for Popular Culture in Recife, which, at the end of the 1950s, set up the cultural circles. According to Paulo Freire, the cultural circles

had no program a priori. The program came about as the result of a consultation with the groups; in other words, the themes would be discussed in the cultural circles; the group would decide. We, as educators, should develop the theme which was to be discussed. But we could add themes, which in *Pedagogy of the Oppressed*, I called "hinge themes"—subjects which would be inserted as fundamental elements in the entire corpus and which would clarify the theme proposed by the people's group. This is because the following happens: there is a popular knowledge, a popular wisdom, which is found in the social practice of the people, but, at times, what is missing is greater solidarity in understanding the themes which make up this knowledge. . .

The positive results which I obtained from this were so considerable on a number of levels—political involvement, understanding, critical reading—that I thought: If it is possible to do this, to reach this level of discussion with popular groups, regardless of their being literate or not, why couldn't it be done within a literacy scheme? Why couldn't the pupils of a literacy scheme become involved politically in the setting up of their system of graphic signs as subjects rather than objects of this system?[3]

This intuition was very important in the latter development of Paulo Freire's work. He had discovered that the form of working, the *process* of the act of learning, was a determining factor in relation to the *content* of learning. It was not possible, for example, to learn how to be a democrat with authoritarian methods.

The participation of the learning subject in the process of the construction of knowledge is not just more democratic, but it proves to be more efficient. Different from the traditional conception of the school, which is based on methods centered on the teacher's authority, Paulo Freire shows that new methods, in which teachers and pupils learn together, are more efficient.

Let us see how he worked in the cultural circles.

Literacy and Conscientization

In the various literacy programs directed by Paulo Freire, the alphabetizer began his work in the field with a notebook, and, if possible, a tape recorder, paying attention to all he saw and read. He mixed with people from the local community as closely as possible. There were no questionnaires or scripts to follow: he asked questions about people's lives and their way of looking at the world. The objective was to make up a list of the words used by the people who would be alphabetized.

FIGURE 3

Cultural circle in Gama, near Brasilia, capital of Brazil,
September 1963.

Everything should be exploited: words, phrases,
expressions, characteristic ways of speaking, of compos-
ing verses, of talking about the world. This preliminary
work on the part of the teacher aimed at revealing the
world lived by the illiterate people, how the thoughts and
the social reality of the group which would be worked with
were presented. Finally, the literacy technique proposed
by Paulo Freire came about as a natural consequence of
the new awareness of the problems lived by the group.[4]

The words and the generative themes, the heart of
the method, resulted from this research work.

The generative words should be chosen by
considering not just their meaning and social relevance
for the cultural circle but also the fact that they had to
present all the phonemes of Portuguese.[5]

These words should *codify* (represent) the way of life of the people from the place. At a later stage, they would be *decodified*, and each word would be associated with a nucleus of questions which were both existential (questions about life) and political (questions about the social factors which determined the conditions of life). For example, for the generative word *government*, the following generative themes could be discussed: political plans, political power, the role of the government in social organization, the participation of the people.[6]

The figurative context gave psychological support to the word in the mind of the illiterate person. The generative word worked as a key. It was presented in a concrete context, as in the classic example of the word brick, where the word is written on a *brick* which forms part of a wall.

Let us look at how a generative word can be used, such as wages.[7]

1. Ideas for discussion: the value of work and its rewards. The use of wages: maintaining the worker and his family. The timetable for work, according to the law. The minimum wage and a just wage. Weekly rest, holidays, bonus salary.

2. Aims of the talk: make the group discuss the situation of the salary of the rural farm workers. Discuss the reason for the situation. Discuss their value and rewards of work. Help the group to discuss the right each of them has to demand a just salary.

3. Steps of the talk: What can you see in this picture? What is the situation of the wages of rural farm workers? Why? What are wages? How much should your wages be? Why? What do you know about the laws about wages? What can we do to get a just wage?

Paulo Freire has insisted that he has never invented any literacy method.

Learning is a process which is part of man, who has a necessity to learn, in the same way he has a necessity to eat. In this process in which man learns about himself and about others, the world acts as a mediator. This is a natural process, which some, like the French educator Decroly, have called a "global process." The experience of Paulo Freire has demonstrated that, in the Portuguese language, no more than some two dozen words are necessary to complete the initial stage of literacy.

What is original in the work of Paulo Freire is the way in which he views this process as a form of achieving freedom. Learning is part of the process of becoming free, of becoming more human.

Whether the coordinator of the circle works with literacy schemes or not, he or she should be a promoting agent of discussion and a careful observer of the difficulties the group has in expression. He should attempt to enable everyone to participate, stimulating them with questions and trying to extend the discussion around the generative word, which should be written in large letters and should be clearly seen by all the pupils. Various teaching resources will be used, from the blackboard to slide projectors and video.

Celso de Rui Beisiegel states:

> Under the stimulus, orientation and control of a "coordinator," the adult is educated through a discussion of his experiences of life with other people who shared the same experiences. In spite of the care with which the reading and writing techniques were planned, with the use of audiovisual resources and a detailed program of activities, the really innovative

elements of the program were: (1) the relationship between the instrumental and the educational action possible during the process; (2) the relationship between the cultural content of the process and the social, political, and economic conditions of the illiterate people.[8]

The Stages of the Method

The method of the formation of a critical conscience passes through three distinct stages. They can be described as follows:

1. Investigation Stage

This is the stage of the discovery of the universe of vocabulary in which the words and generative themes are found which are related to the daily life of the alphabetization pupils and of the social group to which they belong. These generative words are selected according to their syllabic length, their phonetic value, and principally for their social meaning for the group. The discovery of this vocabulary universe can be made through informal meetings with the dwellers of the place in which the scheme will take place—living with them, sharing their worries, and getting a feeling for elements of their culture.

2. Thematization Stage

In this second stage, the themes resulting from the initial awareness stage will be codified and decodified. They will be contextualized and replaced, at first sight magically, by a critical and social vision. In this way, new generative themes are discovered which are related to those which were initially found. It is in this stage that the cards for the breakdown of the phonetic groups are made. These will be of help for reading and writing.

3. Problematization Stage

We can now return from the abstract to the concrete. The limits and possibilities of the existential situations found in the first stage are found. Concrete action becomes necessary which will overcome limiting political, cultural, social, and economic situations, that is, obstacles to *hominization*, the process of becoming men. Being able to read and write becomes an instrument of struggle, social and political activity. The final objective of the method is conscientization. The oppressive reality is experienced as a process which can be overcome. Education for liberation should result in a *transformative praxis*, a collectively organized act of educating with emphasis on the subject.[9]

Literacy of Children

In teaching children how to read and write, the theory is the same, but the process will be very different as the adult's greater use of words and the child's impulse towards play must be taken into account. Asked about the possibility of applying his method to children, Paulo Freire replied:

It is basically about a different vision of educational practice. In the education of children, what is important is not to open their heads to give them the names of islands or historical characters but to allow them to create by getting to know the world and to get to know the world by creating, expressing them-selves and expressing reality, in an increasing ludic understanding of their reality. This is difficult because parents, ideologically controlled by con-sumerism, demand that in schools children consume knowledge. Later, universities transform them into stores of knowledge. Parents demand that schools become supermarkets for their children. But today there are places where we can change this practice.[10]

Literacy for children, however, was not developed by Paulo Freire, but by his daughter, Madalena. Her work was based on the research of Emilia Ferreiro, in addition to the inspiration received from Paulo Freire.[11]

Basic Readers and Cultural Primers

In the second part of the 1950s, Paulo Freire studied a large number of primers, some of them from outside Brazil, in great detail.

His critique of these primers is based on two fundamental premises. The first is that the choice of words, the breakdown of the words into syllables, and the phonetic combination are made by the educator, with the result that the pupil only has to memorize the exercise made for him. The second is that the words and the sounds that are introduced fail to take the child anywhere as they have nothing to do with the life of the children, the region where they live, or the social class to which they belong.

Paulo Freire began from the idea that the process of literacy is an act of creation, of knowledge. What the educator should do when teaching the child is to transform the unilateral act of teaching something to someone into an act of knowing something "by someone and for someone." It is essential that the pupil assume the position of someone who is concretely apprehending the object in order to learn the object. There will be no significant learning if the pupil fails to establish a relationship with the object, if he doesn't act towards it.

As he was against the concept of knowledge assumed by the primers—knowledge coming from outside and being thrown at the pupils—Paulo Freire stopped using them at the end of the fifties and began his experiments without them in the sixties. After a time, however, he discovered that the pupil needed backup material which would fit in with Freire's working philosophy. However, the organization of backup material which would help the pupil in the learning process was not carried out in Brazil due to the military coup. This material would only begin to be organized in Chile, and enriched later by his experience in Africa, where the cultural primers were produced.

The traditional primer, with its ready content to be transferred to the pupil, ignores the formative and creative role which the teacher can play. In the conception of Paulo Freire, the role of the coordinator or the teacher is much more dynamic.

Practice taught Paulo Freire that it is totally useless to make a factory worker, after a tiring day's work, repeat sentences from a reader like "Eva viu a uva (Eva saw the grape); A ave é do Ivo (the bird is Ivo's); A uva é do Ivo (the grape is Ivo's)";—well-known sentences used in traditional forms of alphabetization in Brazil. What does this have to do with his reality?

This principle of reality is equally valid both for adults' and children's learning. One of the first laws of learning is that of interest. As the traditional school presents content which has no interest for pupils—children, teenagers, and adults, it needs to use authoritarian methods in order to teach.

In the cultural primers that Paulo Freire wrote, there is no pure transfer of content to the pupil, though there is content. The fact that the idea of pure transfer of content is rejected doesn't mean that the cultural primers ignore content. Quite the contrary. The content of these readers was studied and developed at length with the objective of building a revolutionary society.

In the 1950s, Paulo Freire spent much time on the question of programmed content. Such a question is as political as it is pedagogical. The great mass of people, educators, and pupils must take part in the discussion on what education is for them and how this should be achieved. This is a central part of the organization of content.

For example, Paulo Freire demonstrated, in one of his cultural primers, that people know how to add because arithmetic is used practically in daily working lives, and that counting has to do with politics. In these readers for people who have became alphabetized, he shows the difference between arithmetic at two moments of the history of São Tomé and Príncipe in the colonial era and after liberation. "Adding" is different from the point of view of the capitalist and the point of view of the worker. The capitalist, in his reckoning, includes a part of the work of the wage earner. But the wage earner can only count on himself and on his workmates. Even arithmetic, which seems so neutral, can be contextualized.

In another primer, on health, abstractions are avoided as the four or five most serious illnesses in the country are presented. Paulo Freire's basic worry in relation to the content of the primers is that they should present the concrete reality to be transformed.

In the cultural primers, the programmed contents are presented in such a way that the pupils take control of them little by little, rather than just receiving them.

Paulo Freire believes that the universalization of material to teach reading is an absurdity from the scientific point of view and an act of authority from the political point of view. In Brazil, educators from the South of the country choose material for the country as a whole. The material ignores the existence of different realities and does not take in the regional and cultural differences of the country. There would also be no sense in gathering educators from all over the country together to elaborate a single text for the whole country. In the same way, it would not be practical to move the center of power to the Northeast as the Northeast would then impose on the South its generative words and themes. Teaching material should be written regionally or even locally.

The Method Nowadays and Its Reinvention

In 1987 Paulo Freire's method was used with considerable success in the first series of municipal schools in Cabo, Olinda, Paulista, Igrassu, and Moreno, all in the state of Pernambuco (Brazil), in a project called "The New School." It could be said that the method was reinvented there as the theories of Emilia Ferreiro on the learning of reading and writing were combined with those of Paulo Freire. In these classes, the emphasis was on the critical spirit and the creativity of the pupil. Traditional primers were not used and the passive behavior of the pupil was not encouraged. Instead of reinforcing in the child the ability to fill in squares and circles in previously prepared material, the child was encouraged to use his inventiveness with a wide range of materials.

In the process of learning how to read and write, the generative words are chosen from the daily vocabulary universe of the pupils, who are encouraged to express themselves verbally. The result is that they are uninhibited, they take part in everything, and that they love the school.

The School of Life project, developed in the town of Cabo, took place along similar lines. It was originally a proposal which aimed at eliminating adult illiteracy. It was set up by Paulo Freire himself, who adapted his method to the socioeconomic reality of the pupils. We can illustrate it by reproducing two texts made by pupils from the postliteracy class and used at a later date in a cultural primer to discuss content and to provide language exercises.

The Challenge of the Road Sweeper.

I found it very difficult to read and write. But now I can write my name and other things.

I'm a road sweeper, a student and a worker. I enjoy studying. I'm learning and I'm going to carry on learning. I have to struggle to learn, I like coming.

The Mayor did something very good for us. It was putting a teacher here with enough patience for us. I thought the challenge of the visit of the supervisor was important. [Joint text from the road sweepers' group]

Tereza

I'm also a pupil from this group. My name's Tereza. Yesterday I had the visit of my father-in-law, who I hadn't seen for three years.

When he saw me giving everyone coffee and getting ready to go out, he asked me: Where are you going, daughter? I said: to school. Does José know about this or do you hide it from him? Not at all, he knows and lets me. Now José has lost his head, where have you seen a woman, already old, who has given birth, thinking about studying?

And I said: father-in-law, times have changed. Nowadays women have their rights. The time when they just lived at the stove has finished. Okay, go on to your school, but come back quick. I'm going, I'll be back at nine.

The father-in-law said: take advantage now because I'm going to talk to José about this school, and I want to see what he has to say. He knows what I'm like and he sees how his mother doesn't even go to the market so as not to learn certain things you find in the heads of some women. And today women are getting very daring. [Women's group from Charneca]

To end this chapter, we must remember one of the central categories in Paulo Freire's work: dialogue.

Dialogue is not just a way to achieve better results; it's not a tactic to make friends or to conquer the pupils. This is manipulation, not dialogue. For Paulo Freire, dialogue is part of human nature. Human beings are constructed through dialogue as they are essentially communicative. There is no human progress without dialogue. For Paulo Freire, the moment of the dialogue is the moment when men meet to transform reality and progress.

Although there is an individual dimension in the process of knowledge, this dimension is not sufficient to explain all the process of knowledge. We need each other to discover. Discovery is a social process, and dialogue is the cement of this process.

Paulo Freire insists on the necessity of dialogue as a teaching strategy. Schools should always listen to what their pupils say about what is taught to them and should be making continuous evaluations. What usually happens is the opposite: they are never asked what they want to learn.

Dialogue is part of this dialogical and dialectic pedagogy, which is today spreading throughout the world, renewing and modernizing educational practices and progress.

3

Learning from History

In 1963, Darcy Ribeiro, Minister of Education in the João Goulart government, asked Paulo Freire to represent the Ministry of Education in SUDENE (Northeast Development Board), whose director was Celso Furtado. Although it was a nonpaid job, it had considerable political importance as its function was to discuss, together with technicians from SUDENE and North American technicians from USAID,[1] the approval of educational projects for the Northeast.

At this time the Alliance for Progress[2] was setting up a number of agreements in the educational area with the state government of Aluísio Alves, in the Northeastern state of Rio Grande do Norte. Paulo Freire was approached by the Secretary of Education, who enquired about the possibility of using his method in Rio Grande do Norte. One of the demands made by Paulo Freire was that the town chosen for the first experiment was not to be visited by the governor during the course in order to avoid electioneering. This demand was not entirely respected.

Historical Factors in the Thinking of Paulo Freire

In 1963 the team, coordinated by the law student Marcos Guerra, went to Natal, the capital of Rio Grande do Norte, to train the group of teachers. Then they went to Angicos to work on the vocabulary universe of the region and to begin their literacy work. After this, the team went to live there. A month later, three hundred formerly illiterate pupils were reading and writing.

The Angicos experience, in which Paulo Freire perfected his method, was publicized throughout Brazil when President João Goulart paid a visit together with all his ministry at the end of the experiment. Paulo Freire was then invited to coordinate the National Literacy Plan. This plan consisted of setting up, in the capital of each state, central teams which would multiply the staff available and put the method into practice. The military coup, however, put a brusque end to all this effort to overcome illiteracy in Brazil.

The experiment in Angicos had been financed by the Alliance for Progress, but, in view of the progressive political content of the work of Paulo Freire, which challenged the colonial and imperialist ideas of the Alliance for Progress, this financial support was withdrawn.

The Northeast of Brazil in the 1950s and the early 1960s was the historical and political environment in which the ideas of Paulo Freire were formed and developed; it was the period of the political crisis which began with the 1930 revolution and which finished with the military coup in 1964.

It was in this period that the popular classes entered the political arena. There were various political groups of different persuasions, among them the radical Catholics, who tried to start a mass mobilization, a consequence of the populism and nationalism of the time.

A series of important events were taking place. The literacy campaign became part of a social context together with the Grassroots Reforms and the growing number of Rural Workers' Leagues.

The Grassroots Reforms consisted of demands of ordinary people which were related to structural, mainly economic, transformations. Among them agrarian reform stood out. This had been the masthead of the social and trade union movements, whose main aim was to question the unproductive *latifundio*. Rural workers, organized in the famous Rural Workers' Leagues, rose up against the existence of these unproductive lands. These Leagues were syndicates which were very active in the hinterland of the states of the Northeast before 1964, when they were banned because of their political activity in favor of landless rural workers. With the attempt to break the control and manipulation of the populist leaders, the possibility arose that the working classes would become aware of their social position and would organize themselves in order to improve their miserable situation.

During all the 1950s and at the beginning of the 1960s, the populist leaders began to lose their ability to manipulate the demands of the masses, who now began to mobilize in rural areas as well as urban areas.

The reply of the great landowners, who, for the first time since the discovery of Brazil, had seen their power questioned, came with the crushing 1964 military coup, which was supported by Brazil's foreign allies.

The Military Coup

At the beginning of the sixties, Paulo Freire could forsee, like the majority of intellectuals, the possibility of a coup. It could be seen in the Brazilian situation, in all the left-wing groups, which "lived a kind of anticipatory idyll with the body of the bride, which was the revolution." There was considerable idealism in the air and some people believed that this process could not be reversed.

After his first experiments to perfect his method, which were made in the MCP, Paulo Freire once confided to Elza that if he continued the work that he was developing, in one or two years he would either be imprisoned or attract the interest of UNESCO (United Nations Educational, Scientific and Cultural Organization) in his research. He was imprisoned in June 1964.

On March 30, 1964, Paulo Freire was taking part in a course in Goiânia when he received a telephone call from his assistant telling him that the news from the federal capital of Brasília was not good and that he should go back to Brasília on the same day. The day after, Miguel Arraes, governor of the state of Pernambuco, was imprisoned, together with the mayor of Recife.

Immediately after the coup, in order to avoid imprisonment, Paulo Freire stayed in the house of a good friend, Luiz Bronzeado, a UDN (National Democratic Union) parliamentary deputy. He stayed in the house and merely waited for time to pass and for the dust to settle. He thought about the possibility of taking refuge in an embassy, but he preferred to stay in Brazil, even though he was sure of the fact that he would be imprisoned, which actually happened, when he and his family went back to Recife.

"Very good, you may be called later to make a statement," the security force chief told him when he voluntarily presented himself. And he was. Early on June 16th, two policemen showed their identification at his door and asked him to accompany them.

As he said in a later statement,[3] in the majority of interrogations, what his questioners tried to prove, as well as his "absolute ignorance (as if there could be an absolute ignorance or wisdom; this only exists in God)," was the danger he represented. He was considered an "international subversive," a "traitor to Christ and the Brazilian people." "Do you deny," one of the judges asked him, "that your method is similar to that of Stalin, Hitler, Perón, and Mussolini? Do you deny that, with your so-called method, you want to make Brazil a bolshevik country?" Later, the process instigated against him was shelved through "ineptness of accusation."

This experience, which lasted seventy days, was sufficiently traumatic to teach him a number of things. In prison, the relationship between education and politics became even clearer to him and confirmed his thesis that social change would have to come from the masses and not from isolated individuals. On the subject of prison, he said that it was possible to learn and educate in the most diverse conditions: as a prisoner, he had something to learn from the experience, even though he might not like it.

After his period in prison, Paulo Freire thought that in such a period of extremes and irrationality, it would be very risky to stay in the country. He said: "I have no vocation to be a hero. I even think that revolutions are made through people that are living and one or two that are dead, not because the heroes wanted them."[4]

Tired of being under rigorous supervision and being called to answer questions and seeing that he wasn't able to do the only thing he could do, and preferring to remain alive instead of giving himself up to a slow death, he opted for exile.

Exile in Chile

At that time, the Bolivian Embassy was the only one which welcomed him. Then he was contacted by the Bolivian Ministry of Education, who sought his help in both child and adult literacy schemes. However, he had difficulty with the altitude of La Paz (twelve thousand feet above sea level), fainting when he arrived. In addition, twenty days after his arrival a coup overthrew the government of Paz Estensoro. Neither he nor other Brazilians in La Paz were affected, but now he was unable to continue living there.

When the coup took place in Brazil in 1964, Chile was getting ready for its September presidential elections. The candidates were Eduardo Frei of the Christian Democratic Party (PDC) and Salvador Allende of the left wing Popular Action Front (FRAP). The right wing withdrew support from its candidate and, fearing the victory of the left, found that it was obliged to support the Christian Democratic candidate, who won the elections.

The PDC started some important reforms, like that of education which, despite all the criticism made of the party's capitalistic modernization platform, resulted in a considerable advance in the democratization of education.

In 1970 Salvador Allende came to power at the head of Popular Unity, with its project for a pacific transition to socialism. Popular Unity was opposed by the Chilean Right and by North American imperialism, which organized opposition to the socialist government and which managed to overthrow Allende through the coup of September 11, 1973.

Paulo Freire lived in Chile from 1964 to 1969, a period in which agrarian reform was begun. This resulted in considerable participation by rural workers in national life. This agrarian reform required a shift of the state apparatus to the countryside to ensure that laws were carried out, that a new agrarian structure could be set up, and that health, transport, credit, technical assistance, schools, and other basic infrastructure services could be provided. The state tried to qualify large numbers of new personnel and technicians to help bring about these changes, mainly in the agricultural sector. Agrarian reform was directly linked to the Ministry of Agriculture and in particular to two organs: the Agricultural Reform Corporation (CORA) and the Institute of Farming and Livestock Development (INDAP), directed by Jacques Chonchol, who became the Minister of Agriculture in Allende's government. INDAP had various subdivisions, including the Social Development Division and the Research and Training Institute for Agrarian Reform (ICIRA), where Paulo Freire worked. Various Brazilian exiles arrived in Chile in 1964 and 1965. These Brazilians managed to find their own niches in the country that welcomed them: in culture, like Thiago de Mello; in academic and intellectual work, like Francisco Weffort and Fernando Henrique Cardoso; in research work like Almino Affonso, author of the work *The Chilean Peasant Movement*; in political attaché work, like Paulo de Tarso Santos and Plínio de Arruda Sampaio; in university work, like the philosopher from Rio Grande do Sul, Ernani Maria Fiori.

The work of Paulo Freire at ICIRA consisted of helping the teams whose task it was to organize small farmers and peasants. His first jobs were to go into the countryside to hear what they had to say and to learn something of the Chilean reality. He was also a consultant for CORA with its literacy schemes and the Ministry of Education with its Adult Education schemes.

The period in exile was extremely important for Paulo Freire.[5] In Chile he found a rich and satisfying political space which was socially and educationally dynamic and which allowed him to restudy his method in other historical circumstances. He was able to reevaluate it in practice and systematize it theoretically.

Educators from the Left supported Paulo Freire's educational philosophy, but he was opposed by the right-wing opposition, which accused him of writing a "very violent" book against Christian Democracy in 1968. This was *Pedagogy of the Oppressed*, which would only be published in 1970. This accusation was one of the factors which made Paulo Freire leave Chile in 1969.

While he was in exile, Paulo Freire gradually began to understand the meaning of the 1964 coup. He thought that a new kind of imperialist intervention had begun in Latin America. It was no longer the obvious domination of the stubborn landowner, who would lower the prices of exported products and keep the workers' wages down. There was a planned project, part of a new political and economic strategy which intended to modernize the economic structure of Brazil and of Latin America and make it more appropriate for capitalist interests and a more subtle, modern, scientific, technological kind of domination. The technology itself which was exported to Brazil under the label of "technical assistance" was, and continues to be, a way of sustaining this domination. This explains the importance Paulo Freire gave, in his work immediately after he left Brazil, to the idea of the "cultural invasion."[6]

If, at the beginning of his exile, he thought he might soon return to Brazil—many people thought the coup was just a temporary uprising by one regiment, which would soon be over—Paulo Freire reached the conclusion that the government which the coup had installed would last longer than his own lifetime. He therefore prepared himself for a long period in exile.

Exile was profoundly educational for Paulo Freire: he began to question Brazil, to understand it better, to understand better what he had done, and to prepare as well as possible to do something outside his own country by making a contribution to another country. Through his experience of cultural differences, he learned the political virtue that was most lacking in Brazil: tolerance, mainly in relation to other cultures. When all is said and done, one culture cannot be called worse than another one.

Elza was never actually exiled. However, she took on the position of an exile to such an extent that she several times refused the offer of a brother who would pay for her to travel to Recife. Her reason was that she could not tread in an airport that was forbidden to her husband. It was a political rather than an existential position.

After a long period in Chile, Paulo Freire, in a conversation with his wife, wondered if, although he was happy in Chile, it might be better for him to leave. His Chilean team had taken over the work he had set up. Besides this, his contract with UNESCO was not renewed, and he had received a number of invitations from North American and European universities.

In 1967 he went to the U.S. for the first time, coordinating seminars in universities in several states. In the U.S. his first, and until then, his only book, *Education as a Practice of Freedom*, had received a considerable amount of publicity.

In 1969 he received a letter from Harvard University inviting him to work there for two years. Eight days later he received a letter from the World Council of Churches in Geneva. This organization had played a very important role when African countries began to rebel against the hegemony of colonial rule and was involved in forms of liberation throughout the continent, supporting organizations like PAIGC of Amílcar Cabral, MPLA in Angola, and FRELIMO in Mozambique.[7] Paulo Freire

FIGURE 4

Strange! In Harvard, Paulo Freire let his beard grow, which changed his face a lot. The motive was the cold. No political or ideological reason.

believed this institution to have considerable historical importance and saw an opportunity of working together with it, as he did for a period of ten years.

Paulo Freire wanted to live the North American experience but by leaving Latin America and working just with books in a library, was afraid of losing contact with the concrete. This would not satisfy him; it would be a kind of alienation. He suggested that he should stay in Harvard for six months and then go to Switzerland. This proposal was accepted. "At that time I was absolutely convinced that it would be fundamental for me to go around the world, to expose myself to various situations, learn from the experience of others and to see myself in different cultural contexts. And this was what the World Council of Churches could give much more than any university."[8]

At Harvard Paulo Freire was a Visiting Professor at the Center of Educational and Developmental Studies, associated with the Center for Studies in Development and Social Change. Here, his book *Cultural Action for Freedom*, which placed cultural action against the imperial cultural invasion, took on its final form.

In Geneva he was a consultant for the World Council of Churches, working as an educational counselor for Third World governments.

From 1970, in a second phase of his exile, in Europe and Africa, the theory and educational practice of Paulo Freire took on a worldwide dimension.

The Main Works of the First Phase of Exile

In the first phase of exile, Paulo Freire wrote his best-known books: *Education as a Practice of Freedom* and *Pedagogy of the Oppressed.*

The first of these unites ideas in a number of articles, lectures, and seminars, within a context of economic development and the movement to overcome the colonial culture. In this society "in transit," Paulo Freire shows the role which education can play in the building of a new, "open," society.

The educational ideas which Paulo Freire develops in this essay, although they may be valid for other societies at other times, are marked by the special conditions of Brazilian society. This society changes rapidly in contradictory directions; it is commanded by an alienated elite, and the ordinary person becomes a mere thing without being aware of it. The key category in this book is that of conscientization, which consists of a liberation process on the part of the dominated conscience to get rid of the influence exercised by the dominating consciousness. The dominated consciousness is "lived in" by the dominator, and the process of conscientization is that of getting rid of this "guest."

While he was working at ICIRA in Chile, Paulo Freire analyzed the question of the "rural extension" and its relationship with previous research. The result was the book *Extensión o comunicación*.[9] In this book, Paulo Freire analyzes the communication between the agricultor and the technician in the agrarian society which is being started. He discusses agrarian reform and change, opposing the concepts *cultural extension* and *cultural communication*. He says that the first idea is one of invasion whereas the second is one of making people aware. He says that the educational action of the agronomist as the teacher should be that of communication if he intends to reach the community. Paulo Freire says that whoever is just "filled" by others, with just content that contradicts his own way of being, does not learn. The agronomist-educator who is not aware of the world view of the peasant cannot change his behavior. Here, Paulo Freire's interest is in emphasizing the principles and stating the bases of education as a practice for freedom. This education is not that of mere technical ability but includes the importance of the human being.

In the other book he worked on while in Chile, *Pedagogy of the Oppressed*,[10] Freire shows the oppressive mechanisms of capitalist education. He begins by discussing the historical development of the dominated consciousness and its dialectic relationship with the dominating consciousness. Covering all that he had said up to then on the topic of education, it is Freire's most important and extensive work. It is the result of his first five years of exile and fruit of educational work in various concrete situations rather than, as Paulo Freire admits in the first lines of the work, intellectual fancies or simple book reading. The book is dedicated to "radical nonsectarians."

This work is based on the dialectics of the unity between subjectivity and objectivity, between past and future, between previous and new knowledge. He believes that sectarianism belongs to reactionaries while radicalization is appropriate for the revolutionary.

Cultural Action for Freedom[11] was published after his exile in Chile. In this work, Paulo Freire shows the impossibility of dialogue between antagonists, as this dialogue would suppose equality of conditions and reciprocity. He refers particularly to the neocolonial relations already existing between the "mother-countries" of the First World and the countries of the so-called Third World.

African Experience

The second phase of exile begins with Paulo Freire's move to Geneva in 1970.

The following year, a group of Brazilian exiles founded IDAC (Institute for Cultural Action), a research and educational center directed toward real and concrete situations and whose base was that of conscientization as a revolutionary factor in education and in society.

FIGURE 5

Paulo Freire beside Miguel Darcy de Oliveira, from IDAC, and
Mário Cabral, Minister of Education, in Guinea-Bissau, in 1978.

Its political and educational direction was that of
attempting to build, in every concrete situation, a
pedagogy of the oppressed. In other words, through

undergoing an educational practice in which, based on the realities and the interests of those with whom one works, one looks for a process of knowledge and ways in which one can change reality.

As president of the executive committee of IDAC, Paulo Freire decided that he should just participate for a limited time, so that the group could grow without depending on him.

At one time, IDAC received so many requests that it ran the risk of becoming an institute that just ran seminars. However, in 1975 there was a great opportunity for it to find its proper place: Mário Cabral, minister of Education in the Republic of Guinea-Bissau, invited Paulo Freire and his IDAC team to visit his country and contribute to the development of the national literacy scheme.

Guinea-Bissau, a former Portuguese colony, is a small country in West Africa whose eight hundred thousand inhabitants are mainly peasants. It experienced a fifteen-year exemplary war of national liberation.

It was Paulo Freire's first experience of Africa. African time is different. The letters that IDAC sent Mário Cabral[12] didn't receive prompt replies, due to the struggle the government was undergoing. In the intervals between the letters, the personnel from IDAC read the texts of Amīlcar Cabral and talked with people who had been in Guinea-Bissau.

The necessity that their experiment should not interfere in the revolutionary process in Guinea-Bissau was discussed. It was important to forget what had happened in previous literacy schemes so that this previous work would not be given a universal value which then would be transferred to Guinea-Bissau.

Working coherently with its proposal, IDAC didn't go to Guinea-Bissau as an international expert in people's

FIGURE 6

The 1st National Literacy Seminar, Monte Mário, Democratic
Republic of São Tomé and Príncipe, 1976.

education but went in order to collaborate as a militant.
Its members took no ready-made projects to prescribe to
the government which had invited them. If this had been
the case, they would have been behaving like neocolon-
ialists. IDAC rejected this line completely and followed the
idea that experiences are lived and not transplanted.

From the assistance that was given there was an
enormous amount of learning, both on the part of those
who were teaching and those who were learning. The
dramatic lack of material resources, the limited efficiency
of certain coordinators of the cultural circles, who needed
more thorough training, and the vestiges of the old
ideology interfering in the developmental process of the
country were all noted down, studied, and thought about.

In the texts of Amílcar Cabral and in his experience in exile, Paulo Freire lived the dialectic between patience and impatience. He had to be patient, impatiently. It was necessary to be impatient, patiently. He said that the exile who fails to learn this lesson is lost. If this connection is broken, if he tends to be more patient, this characteristic becomes an anaesthetic which takes him to dreams which cannot be fulfilled. If he tends to be excessively impatient, this will lead him to a super-activity, a voluntariness and eventually to disaster. The only solution is a *contradictory harmony.*

In September 1975 Paulo Freire took part in an international symposium in Iran which had, at this time, an enormous repercussion. In the final text, called the Declaration of Persepolis, the relationship between literacy campaigns and the involvement of people in sociopolitical changes was clarified.

Between 1975 and 1978 Paulo Freire worked in São Tomé and Príncipe, not as a technician but as a militant educator who tried not to separate his task from the liberation cause of the oppressed. This country, recently released from the Portuguese colonial yoke, gave him the confidence of its revolutionary leadership and proposed to him that he should develop a literacy program. The results were much better than expected. Four years later, Paulo Freire received a letter from the Minister of Education, who said that 55 percent of all those enrolled and that 72 percent of those who had finished the course had become literate. In the commemoration ceremony that followed, a man who had recently become literate wrote a message in his own hand.

Also in the 1970s, a number of the most prestigious universities in the world awarded him honorary doctorates: the Open University in Great Britain, Louvain in

Belgium, the University of Michigan, and the University of Geneva. In addition, Paulo Freire accepted invitations to work in Australia, Italy, Angola, Nicaragua, the Fiji Islands, India, Tanzania, and in numerous other countries.

The homage from the University of Geneva, where he kept a seminar going on popular education, was one of the last acts he took part in before being amnestied and returning to Brazil, after fifteen years in exile. In spite of the many invitations he had received during this period, he could never enter Brazil as he was always refused an entry visa.

On August 7, 1979, he went to Brazil for a month's visit. Immediately after, he returned to Geneva to discuss with his family, IDAC, and the World Council of Churches his definitive return to Brazil, which was made in March 1980.

4

A Pedagogy for Liberation

Paulo Freire is, without a shadow of doubt, a humanistic and militant educator. His conception of education always comes from solutions that are found from a concrete context. In *Education as a Practice of Freedom*, this context is the economic-development process and the movement to overcome the colonial culture in the "societies in transition." The author attempts to show what the role of education in these societies is from the point of view of ordinary people in the construction of a democratic society or an "open society." This kind of society cannot be constructed by the elites since they are incapable of providing the bases for political reforms. This new society can only be the result of the struggle of the popular masses, who are the only ones who can make such a change.

Paulo Freire believes that it is possible to both engage people politically and educate them in this process of conscientization and mass movement. In the book I have just mentioned, he develops the notion of *transitive critical conscience*, understanding it as the conscience which is articulated with the praxis. To reach this conscience, which is both challenging and transforming, critical dialogue, talk, and experience of living together are necessary.

Dialogic Pedagogy

The dialogue proposed by the elites is vertical; it forms the mass of those who are educated and prevents them from showing what they think. In this supposed dialogue, the person who is being educated only needs to listen and obey. In order to pass from the stage of ingenuous conscience to critical conscience, it is necessary to follow a long path, along which he who is being educated will reject the oppressor who has been "living" inside him. The fact that the oppressor has been living inside him makes the pupil feel ignorant and incapable. This is the path toward his self-affirmation as an individual.

In Paulo Freire's conception, dialogue is a horizontal relationship. It is fed by love, humility, hope, faith, and confidence. It takes on the traditional characteristics of the dialogue with new formulations through the course of many kinds of work contextualizing them. For example, he refers to the experience of the dialogue when insisting that democracy should be practiced in public schools: "It's necessary to have the courage to make democratic experiments."[1]

The first virtue of dialogue consists of respect for those who are being educated, not only as people but also in the way they are considered examples of social practice. This has nothing to do with spontaneity, which hands the pupils over to themselves. Spontaneity, Paulo Freire said on this occasion, has only helped the right wing up to now. The presence of the educator is much more than a shadow of the presence of the pupils; indeed, there is no attempt to deny the authority which the educator has and represents.

The differences between the educator and the pupil are found in "a relationship in which the freedom of the pupil is allowed to be expressed." This statement is more political than pedagogical and makes the educator a politician and an artist and not someone who is neutral.

On this particular occasion, he remembered that another fundamental virtue is to listen to the urgencies and the choices of the pupil. He concluded by remembering another virtue: that of tolerance, which is the "virtue of living with what is different in order to be able to argue with what is antagonistic."

As can be seen, for Paulo Freire, education is part of the process of humanization. This idea appeared in his first works, such as the article "The Role of Education in Humanization," published in 1969.[2]

On the other hand, Paulo Freire, as we saw in his historical method, has a dialectic way of thinking, by not separating practice and theory as positivists do. Theory, method, and practice form a whole in his work, which is guided by the relationship between knowledge and the knower. This whole forms a theory of knowledge and an anthropology in which knowledge has an emancipating role.

His work *Pedagogy of the Oppressed* completed his pedagogical conceptions on the differences between the pedagogy of the colonizer and the pedagogy of the oppressed. Here, his vision of class appears more clearly: "The bourgeois pedagogy of the colonizer is the 'bank' pedagogy." The awareness of the oppressed is "immersed" in the world which was prepared by the oppressor; from there there exists a *duality* in the minds of the oppressed: on one side there is an adherence to the oppressor, this "living" of the conscience of the dominator (his values, his ideology, his interests) inside the oppressed, together with the fear of being free, and, on the other hand, the wish and need to free himself. So, in the minds of the oppressed there is an internal struggle which needs to move from being individual to being collective: "Nobody frees anybody else; nobody is freed alone; people free themselves together."

Banking Education and Problematizing Education

With his thesis on the relationship between education and the process of humanization, Paulo Freire characterizes two opposing conceptions of education: the banking conception and that of Paulo Freire.

In the banking conception (bourgeois), it is the educator who knows and the pupils who don't; it is the educator who thinks and the pupils who are "thought"; it is the educator who speaks and the pupils who quietly listen; it is the educator who makes and prescribes his choice and the pupils who follow his prescription; it is the educator who chooses the content of the program; the pupils' ideas on the program are never heard, and they have to get used to it. The educator gives himself the authority of his function, which has the authority of knowledge, and this is antagonistic to the freedom of the pupils, who have to adapt to the determinations of the educator. Finally, the educator is the subject of the process while the pupils are mere objects.

In the banking conception, narrative and dissertative relationships predominate. Education becomes an act of depositing (as in banks); "knowledge" is a donation from those who know to those who don't know anything.

Banking education has as its aim the maintenance of the division between those who know and those who don't know, between the oppressors and the oppressed. It denies the possibility of dialogue, while problematizing education (the method of Paulo Freire) is founded on the dialogical and dialectical relationship between the educator and the pupil: both learn together.

Dialogue is, however, an existential demand, which enables communication and allows what is immediate and at hand to be surpassed. Surpassing these "situation-limits," the pupil-educator reaches a complete vision of the context. This should take place from the time of the setting-up of the program, the generative themes, the understanding of the contradictions, to the last stage of the development of each study.

In order to put this dialogue into practice, the educator cannot put himself in the ingenuous position of someone who intends to possess all knowledge but should first put himself in the position of someone who knows that he doesn't know everything and recognize that the illiterate is not "lost," out of reality, but someone who has his own experience of life and who therefore has knowledge.

In a dialogue with Sérgio Guimarães,[3] Paulo Freire refers to the dialogic category not just as a method but as a strategy to respect the knowledge of the pupil who arrives at the school. He remembers an incident that happened to him with an ecclesiatical grassroots community in the outskirts of Belo Horizonte when the Education Secretariat was consulting the population in the Minas Gerais Education Congress. One of those present said, "They never ask us what we want to learn. It's the opposite, they always tell us what we should study." Paulo Freire replied, "But what is studying?" The teenager who had asked the question answered, "First, you don't study just at school but in everyday life. Two men were traveling in a truck full of fruit. Suddenly they came to a very muddy part of the road. The driver stopped. The two got down. They tried to improve the situation. They went through the mud trying to tread lightly. Then, they discussed the situation. They gathered some dry branches and stones and lined the road. They finally managed to get through the mud without any difficulty. These men studied. Studying is also this.

After this speech, other participants began to criticize the school for not giving enough attention to the rights of the workers. Paulo Freire concluded that what is most important is the realization that the pupils, when they arrive at school, also have something and are not there just to listen.

Dialogic and Antidialogic Theory

In chapter 4 of *Pedagogy of the Oppressed*, Paulo Freire analyzes the theories of cultural action, which are developed from the antidialogic and dialogic frameworks.

In his analysis of the antidialogic theory, he emphasizes the following characteristics:

1. The necessity of *conquest*, which is an essential act of the antidialogic theory. The "content and methods of conquest vary historically; what does not vary, while there is a dominating elite, is the necrophiliac anxiety to oppress."
2. The *division for domination*, to keep people in a state of immersion in their own reality, which consists of "dividing the oppressed, creating and deepening the differences between them through a wide variety of methods and processes."
3. Manipulation; another instrument of conquest: "an imperious necessity of the dominating elites, which aims at reaching an inauthentic type of 'organization'; this avoids its opposite, which is the true organization of the immersed and emerging popular masses."

4. Cultural invasion, which consists of the "penetration of the invaders in the cultural contexts of individual beings, imposing on them the invaders' vision of the world and preventing the creativity of individual beings from finding an outlet."

In his analysis of dialogic theory, Paulo Freire emphasizes the characteristics which are diametrically opposed to those of the antidialogic theory: (1) collaboration, (2) union, (3) organization, and (4) cultural synthesis.

The revolutionary educator cannot use the same methods and antidialogic procedures which serve the oppressors:

> In the same way that the oppressor, in order to oppress, needs a theory of oppressive action, the oppressed, in order to achieve freedom, equally need a theory appropriate for their action. The oppressor elaborates a theory of action, which will necessarily be without the people, as he is against them. The people, on the other hand, crushed and oppressed, introjecting the oppressor, cannot make their theory of liberating action alone. Only in the meeting with revolutionary leadership, in the joining of both, in the praxis of both, can this theory be made and remade.[4]

Paulo Freire links education to the struggle and class organization of the oppressed. For him, the oppressed class is larger than the working class. It is only from the beginning of capitalism that one can correctly talk about social classes. It was capitalism that gave social classes a clear shape though one cannot say, however, that there were no oppressors and oppressed before capitalism. But Paulo Freire goes a step further: oppression can also be found with the oppressed themselves.

The Directive Role of the Educator

Paulo Freire does not ignore the directive and informative role of education, the educational relationship of the act of knowledge. He nevertheless insists that knowledge cannot be confused with truth, as is found in positivistic theories of knowledge. It is necessary to elaborate a new theory of knowledge, beginning with the interests of the oppressed, which will allow them to reelaborate and reorder their own knowledge and, using this framework, allow them to obtain hitherto unknown knowledge.

In this new theory of discovery, the knowledge that is most important for the liberation of the oppressed is that of gaining awareness of their own situation of being oppressed, which is seen in the political oppression and the economic exploitation which they live under. But this awareness cannot take place abstractly. Awareness is achieved in the practice of the oppressed people organizing themselves.

Paulo Freire has been questioned several times as to whether his dialogic theory of knowledge and education might give free rein to spontaneity and nondirectivity. In order to dissipate any doubt, he clarified this point in a dialogue with Moacir Gadotti and Sérgio Guimarães:

> I have never said that the educator is the same as the pupil. Quite the contrary, I have always said that whoever says that they are equal is being demagogic and false. The educator is different from the pupil. But this difference, from the point of view of the revolution, must not be antagonistic. The difference becomes antagonistic when the authority of the educator, different from the freedom of the pupil, is

transformed into authoritarianism. This is the demand I make of the revolutionary educator. For me, it is absolutely contradictory when the educator, in the name of the revolution, takes power over the method and orders the pupil, in an authoritarian way, using this difference that exists. This is my position, and therefore it makes me surprised when it is said that I defend a nondirective position. How could I defend the fact that the nature of the educational process is always directive whether the education is given by the bourgeoisie or the working class.[5]

Paulo Freire takes up the theme of the directivity of the teacher to reply to a question from the North American educator Ira Shor, on the right of the educator to change the consciousness of the pupils. Respecting the pupil does not mean leaving him ingenuous. It means assuming his ingenuousness together with him, in order to overcome it. The revolutionary educator, he says, should not manipulate his pupils, but should also not leave them to their own fate: "The opposite is laissez-faire or the refusal of the responsibility that the teacher has toward education." This directivity is not a position of someone who orders someone else to do something, but that of someone who directs tasks and a serious study. "I call this a radically democratic position," he continues, "because it demands directivity and freedom at the same time, with no authoritarianism from the teacher and no licentious freedom from the pupils."[6]

Moving from the directive nature of all education, Paulo Freire distinguishes the liberating directive educator from the domesticating directive educator.

The first shows the reality of the syllabus by uncovering the raison d'être of the object of study and by establishing an atmosphere of camaraderie in the classroom. The second type denies reality, falsifies it, trying to reduce it to what he thinks of it and tries to convince the pupil that, for example, a table is a chair; he doesn't listen, he has no sensitivity, he doesn't communicate; he only makes communications.

Naturally, teacher and pupil are not the same—the teacher gives marks and sets tasks. His critical competence is different from that of the pupils. For the liberating educator, concludes Paulo Freire, "these differences are not antagonistic, as they are in authoritarian classrooms. The liberating difference is a tension which the teacher tries to overcome through a democratic attitude toward his own directivity."[7]

The authoritarian teacher dehumanizes rather than humanizes. He never asks the pupils to think and to make a fresh reading of their reality. On the contrary, he presents it as something already complete and finished, to which it is enough simply to adapt. No transformation is experienced. Instead of suggesting to the pupils that they control the knowledge they have, he proposes merely the passive reception of packaged knowledge.

On the other hand, the liberating educator will invite the pupils to think. To be aware, is not, in this sense, a simple formula or a mere slogan. It is, in the words of Paulo Freire, "a radical form of being of human beings as human beings who, remaking the world which they didn't make, make their world, and in this making and remaking, they remake themselves. They are because they are being."

This very dense formulation of the relationship between education and humanization was made at the International Symposium for Literacy, in Persepolis, Iran, in September 1975. Paulo Freire concludes:

Just reading "Eva viu a uva" (Eva saw the grape) mechanically is not enough. It is also necessary to understand the position that Eva occupies in her social context, who works to produce grapes and who makes profit from this work.

The defenders of the neutrality of literacy programs do not lie when they say that the clarification of reality at the same time as learning to read and write is a political act. They are wrong, however, when they deny that the way in which they deny reality has no political meaning.[8]

The Intellectual and the Popular Masses

In his book *Education and Change*, Paulo Freire discusses the role of the intellectual and the technician, saying that, if on the one hand, every radical transformation implies a "lucid vanguard," it is also necessary, on the other hand, that such a transformation is nurtured in dialogue with the popular masses and that the intellectual and the technician get to know them so that, with them, it can fulfill what is "historically viable." Paulo Freire also criticizes the false dilemma between humanism and the technical element of education: "An education that is opposed to taking advantage of the technical ability of people is as inefficient as that which is reduced to technical competence with no general humanistic education."

In a dialogue with Antonio Faundez, Paulo Freire refers to the relationship between the militant political intellectual and the popular masses: "The militant political intellectual will always run the risk of either becoming authoritarian or of intensifying his authoritarianism if he is incapable of overcoming a messianistic conception of revolutionary social transformation." He quotes Che Guevara and Amílcar Cabral, who never gave up holding gatherings with the people and adds, "In reality, the position that defends gatherings with the people is not that of folding one's arms, it is not that of he who thinks that the role of the intellectual is just that of an assistant, a helper, a facilitator." His role is to place his ability at the disposal of the people: "The intellectual must know that his critical ability is neither superior or inferior to that of popular feeling. One requires both in order to read reality."[9] For the pedagogy of Paulo Freire, there is no dichotomy between feeling the fact and learning its reason for being.

Several pages later, he remembers Marx's angry words against the reluctance of the bourgeois intellectuals to learn with the popular masses when he wrote to a friend: "We can't therefore march with men who openly declare that workers are too uncultivated to emancipate themselves, so that they will have to be liberated from above by philanthropists from the great bourgeoisie and the petty bourgeoisie."[10]

Because of this, Paulo Freire has insisted that the pedagogy of the oppressed is also a pedagogy of questioning that can be lived both in school and in the political struggle. It is a pedagogy that is strongly democratic and anti-authoritarian and which is never that of spontaneity or liberal conservatism.

Cultural Action for Freedom

As I have previously said, education for Paulo Freire is a moment of the transformation of man mediated by the transformation of the world. Based on this framework, he develops a considerable body of work which extends well beyond the limits of pedagogy, taking in the areas of economics, politics, and social sciences. From his theoretical framework, other people have developed works through "applications" and studies. Paulo Freire's own production has been considerable. His works show his theoretical evolution and, most importantly, his preoccupation with practical proposals.

In *Extensão ou comunicação?* Paulo Freire discusses his theory of knowledge, basing himself on four dimensions: the *logical* (related to methods of knowledge), the *historical* (referring to the relationship between knowledge and context), the *gnosiologic* (referring to the ends of knowledge), and the *dialogic* (referring to the communication of knowledge). Freire pays greatest attention to the last: the thinking subject doesn't think alone.

Paulo Freire believes that communication should be simple. Everything that is understood, even if it is complex, should be expressed simply. But simplicity has nothing to do with simplisms. "By using simplicity one can go deeply into things in an accessible, uncomplicated way. With simplisms, one stays on the outside of the object one is examining, and above all, one fails to treat the object seriously."

In *Cultural Action for Freedom*, Paulo Freire extends the ideological analysis of the dominant education and denounces its pseudoneutrality and astuteness. He analyzes literacy programs and shows that this ideology can be seen in the expressions that are used, such as, for example "weed," "illness," "inability of the people," and "eradication of illiteracy."

The words and expressions used in teaching textbooks provide us with a good example of the underlying ideology. The children of working-class people are often called "inferior," "failures," or "with no future." Paulo Freire once made—in a lecture given at the Catholic University of São Paulo in 1984, during the course "The

Church and Power"—an analysis of daily language to show that we reveal traces of authoritarianism and of racism in our discourse. Power, he said, the power of the white race, which considers itself to be superior, is also expressed through racism. Brazil is racist, although many people speak of an "ethnic democracy." This is no more than a myth. If you ask somebody, for example: "Do you know Maria?" the other person will reply, "I do. She's a little nigger (pretinha)... but she's great!"

Paulo Freire made the following comments on this dialogue. Firstly, a diminutive, *pretinha* for *preta*, is used as a sweetener, and this sweetener is racist. Secondly, in addition to the diminutive pretinha, the phrase referred to has a *but*, a conjunction of contrast. Why the *but*? No one would say, "I know so-and-so. She's a little blond girl, she's got lovely blue eyes... but." And he ends, "We learn at school what a conjunction is, but we don't learn about the ideology of the conjunction, that it expresses the question of power."

These frequently exhaustive analyses are very frequent in the work of Paulo Freire. As a former teacher of Portuguese, he gives an enormous amount of attention to expression, whether it is oral or written. He always tries to discover what it covers up. In the classroom he never lets any example of hidden prejudice pass. In this way he continues to teach and educate.

In *Cultural Action for Freedom*, Paulo Freire reelaborates his theory of knowledge by contrasting *theory* to *verbalism* and *action* to *activism*. He considers that the unity of theory and practice is essential for an educational act that will lead in the direction of freedom. On the other hand, he tries to demystify the concept of conscientization (which became widespread from his first work), in the sense in which it is used by the dominant ideology: conscientization is understood as "conscience of action over" reality and not as "a taking of consciousness." Conscientization takes place in reality, not in theory.

"Cultural action" and "cultural revolution" are two moments of the liberating action: the first takes place in opposition to the dominating classes, and the second takes place after the political and social revolution. He says:

There is one revolutionary kind of education before and another after the revolution has been established. At the beginning, it can't be made inside the power bases as these power bases will silence everything, but it should take place inside popular social movements like unions and nonpopulist popular political parties. And it is through the educators that the traitor pedagogues make their conversion from one side to another, their class suicide. When the revolutionary cry is in power, then revolutionary education will take on another dimension: what was before an education to contest and challenge becomes a systematized education, re-creating, helping the reinvention of society. In the previous phase, it helped the call to overthrow a power which was hostile to the masses; now on the side of the masses, education becomes an extra-ordinary instrument to help build a new society and a new man.[11]

Christian Socialism and Utopia

The practical teaching to which Paulo Freire has devoted himself since his youth is very connected to his religious feeling.

He says that, once, when he was still very young, he went to the canals and hills in the rural backwaters near Recife compelled by a "certain pleasant and daring intimacy with Christ" and full of a "sweetly Christian" vision. Once there, the dramatic and challenging reality of the people took him back to Marx, who didn't prevent him from finding Christ in the alleys.

As a left-wing thinker, Paulo Freire believes that being a Christian does not mean being a reactionary and that being a Marxist does not mean being an inhuman bureaucrat. Christians should reject exploitation.

This is the way in which his work started, gaining strength from the Christian socialist movement of the sixties and seventies. The political consciousness of this movement made him realize that he had become a politician through being an educator and a Christian. It was impossible for him to be neutral as a Christian, in the same way that it was impossible for him to be neutral as an educator.

Paulo Freire's thinking is utopian but not in the sense that it can definitively never be fulfilled. For him, utopia is not idealism: "it is the dialectics of the acts of denunciation and annunciation, it is the act of denouncing the dehumanizing structure and of announcing the humanizing structure. For this reason, too, utopia is also a historical commitment."[12]

On the subject of utopia, Diana Cunha has made the following comments:

> In his definition of what is utopian, Paulo Freire, as well as valuing utopia as viable for human beings, is aware of its historical presence. In other words, being utopian is to deny an inhuman present and one should get involved in the struggle for a more human

future. What is contained in utopia is only a planned project, which will only become a project as part of historical action, which is where it becomes viable and real. Between utopia and its fulfillment there is a *historical time*, which is the time of the transforming action, of the construction of our reality. Only utopias can be prophetic, giving us hope. And only those utopias that denounce and announce can be prophetic—the oppressors will never be prophetic as they wish to change nothing in favor of the rest.[13]

5

Relearning Brazil

A year before receiving amnesty, Paulo Freire had been invited to return to Brazil to take part in the First Seminar of Brazilian Education, but once again, he was refused a passport.

The organizers of the seminar, which took place in Campinas, managed to get past the censor by presenting a recorded telephone message from Paulo Freire to the eight hundred participants. In this message, he spoke of the enormous nostalgia he felt for the smell and taste of Brazil, from which he was far, but from which he would never be far.

After obtaining a court order, he managed to get the passport which had been systematically denied him by various Brazilian consulates in a number of countries. After fifteen years in exile, he returned at the age of fifty-seven, arriving at Viracopos Airport in Campinas. When asked if he had been following the political and educational development of Brazil, he said he had done the impossible in order to do so and added, "But at each moment I find that you must be here to understand our present reality better. Fifteen years' absence demands learning and a greater intimacy with the Brazil of today. I have come back to relearn Brazil."

Exile hadn't left him with bitterness or excessive homesickness. His return, an important moment in the

FIGURE 7

Paulo Freire returns to Brazil after 16 years in exile and visits the Education and Society Center of Studies (CEDES), in Campinas, São Paulo State. From left to right: Maurício Tragtenberg, Carlos Rodrigues Brandão and Moacir Gadotti.

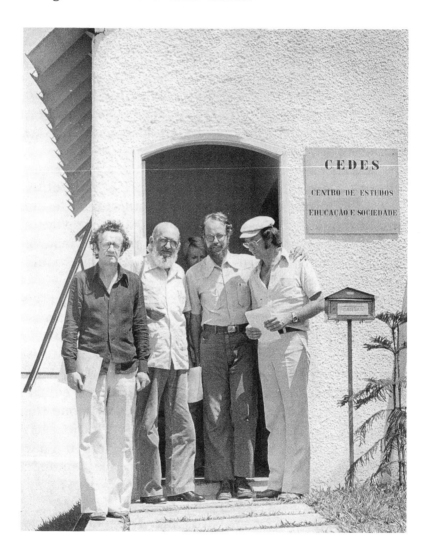

he would be interested in working there. He immediately accepted. The director of the Faculty of Education, Eduardo Chaves, took advantage of the fact that a teacher had left to propose the name of Paulo Freire. However, the rector of the university withheld his approval, and only after protests from both academics and students was Paulo Freire contracted. At the same time, he began to work in the Postgraduate Education program at the Catholic University of São Paulo.

When he was still in exile, he was one of the founders of CEDES (Center for the Study of Education and Society), which started, together with the journal *Educação e sociedade* (Education and society), during the First Seminar of Brazilian Education in 1978.

In 1981 he helped to found Vereda, the Center for Studies in Education, in São Paulo. This center was responsible for research, assistance, and training of teachers who would work in the area of popular education.

One of the ways in which Paulo Freire relearned Brazil was through his participation in teachers' movements and popular education movements, for example, the discussion with teachers from the state of Minas Gerais, which took place in April 1981, and more especially, his participation in the struggle of the working class. This involvement with the working class had a profound repercussion in the works which he wrote after his exile.

In this discussion, Paulo Freire touched on various subjects such as the hunger found in the misery of the region where he grew up and how his familiarity with Marx had not broken his relationship with Christ. He also examined the fact that the power of manipulation and domestication of Brazilian television has produced alienating, inaccessible dreams for the dominated class

and the fact that television was hand-in-hand with
authoritarianism. In addition, he encouraged teachers to
propose to their pupils that they should choose between
letting themselves be manipulated by the teacher,
accepting the syllabus imposed by him, and participating
as subjects in the setting up of their own programs, taking
their education into their own hands. He concluded, "The
transformation of education cannot take place before the
transformation of society, but this transformation of
society needs education."[1]

A New Context, New Ideas

Paulo Freire's relearning can also be seen in the large
number of texts published by him and about him. We can
emphasize the most important which are related to
education and the training of the educator. What is
important is not just the account of this relearning but
also the process itself. Many of these authors have shared
experiences with him and share the same practice and
theory of education. Paulo Freire has frequently reaffirmed the importance of writing and rewriting with his
colleagues, highlighting the production and renewal in
various contexts of the pedagogy of the oppressed as a
collective work.

He greatly values young educators and takes part in
projects with them which are also a source of a permanent
learning.

Let us see how this process of relearning has taken
place.

In 1979 the Brazilian edition of *Educação e mudança*
was released. This book was an analysis of the possibilities of the educational system in the process of social
change. In this work, Paulo Freire develops the idea of a

commitment as a category in the pedagogical act. It is a political commitment, but it also takes in the technical and professional training of the pupil. He also clearly schematizes the characteristics of the ingenuous conscience. This book, whose publication in Brazil coincided with his return to the country, was translated by myself and Lilian Lopes Martins. I also wrote the preface, in which I discuss the relationship between dialogue and conflict, starting from the presupposition that merely dialogue is not sufficent for a transformative pedagogy in a class society. Together with other educators, among them Rubem Alves, Marilena Chaui, Carlos Rodrigues Brandão, Vanilda P. Paiva, and Luiz Eduardo Wanderley, Freire published *A Questão política da educação popular* in 1980, in which popular education is not only linked to the popular classes but also to socialism.

Works on Paulo Freire

Sílvia Maria Manfredi wrote *Política e educação popular* (1981), in which she presents the economic, political, and educational characteristics of the beginning of the sixties, Paulo Freire's method, and the way it has been used in educational experiments. She examines themes which help the professional development of teachers in all the areas of teaching in the first, second, and third grades.

Although he has worked with communication and culture, this area of Paulo Freire's work has been given little attention. In *Communicação e cultura: as idéias de Paulo Freire*, Venício Artur de Lima (1981) describes the social context of Freire's ideas, their importance for communication studies, works by and about Paulo Freire, and Freire's concept of communication and of culture, which takes into account the dialectic nature of their language.

Wagner Gonçalves Rossi (1982), in *Pedagogia do trabalho: caminhos da educação socialista,* selects material and authors, giving preference to those least known to a Brazilian audience (Makarenko and Freinet), briefly discusses John Dewey, Gramsci, Snyders and Nidelcoff, makes a more detailed study of Pistrak and gives a chapter to Paulo Freire, including a simple, descriptive section which was originally written for the North American reader. Rossi places Paulo Freire in the development of the history of socialist pedagogy. Rossi calls this the pedagogy of work as all the educationalists he analyzes see work as a fundamental category. Makarenko believes in the value of manual work and even builds machines with his students. Similarly, Freinet and Dewey value work as a basic methodological element in learning. Dewey affirms, "It is necessary to learn by doing." In the other authors Rossi analyzes, work is an anthropological principle of education. This means that education trains men, but it is man himself who is responsible for his training. He constructs himself, producing his own material and spiritual existence.

The vicissitudes of Paulo Freire's ideas and pedagogical practice are the object of the analysis of Celso de Rui Beisiegel, in *Política e educação popular: a teoria e a prática de Paulo Freire no Brasil,* published in 1982. The author describes how the ideas that inspired the social action of the Brazilian Catholic Church, the national-developmentalist ideas which were formulated at ISEB, the bases of Anglo-Saxon liberal democracy and his educational practice with the popular masses of Recife were the starting points for Paulo Freire in the creation of his literacy and conscientization method.

Between 1979 and 1981, the Loyola publishing company released three books on Paulo Freire, written by Carlos Alberto Torres: Consciência e História: *a práxis educativa de Paulo Freire, Diálogo com Paulo Freire*, and *Leitura Crítica de Paulo Freire*. Torres emphasizes the anthropological and methodological aspects of Paulo Freire. In one of his theses, he examines the relationship between Hegelian dialectics and the philosophy of problematizing education. He concludes that the difference is in the concept of auto-conscience. In Hegel, it is idealistic and subjectivistic. In Paulo Freire, it is integrated into the conscience of the Other. According to the philosopher Eliseu Cintra in his thesis, "The Sense of the Other in Paulo Freire," the other can be seen in three ways: (1) through an ethical choice for the value of the Other as a person, in his individuality; (2) by considering the Other as someone who gives meaning to me myself, completing me as a human being; (3) through dialogue, in which I open myself to the Other, becoming receptive to him. This concept of alternity comes from Christianity, and it is in this way that conscientizing education tries to overcome antidialogicism.

In 1986, the Ecuadorian educator Rosa Maria Torres, today consultant to UNICEF (New York), carried out an important study on Paulo Freire, based on an interview with him. She situated Freire's theory and practice in their historical context both in Brazil and in other countries in Latin America. This study was published in 1987 under the title *Educação popular: um encontro com Paulo Freire*. Similar to the works of Marcela Gajardo and Carlos Alberto Torres, Rosa Maria Torres has helped to demystify and give permanent value to the work of Paulo Freire.

Peter McLaren (1989) of Miami University wrote a book on critical pedagogy and educational foundations with the title *Life in Schools: An Introduction to Critical Pedagogy in the Foundations of Education.* He identifies liberation pedagogy as a significant trend within the broader perspective of critical pedagogy, and places Paulo Freire alongside renowned critical educators such as Jonathan Kozol, John Dewey, Michael Apple, and Henry Giroux.

In 1990, Carlos Alberto Torres published *The Politics of Nonformal Education in Latin America* in which the author, Professor at the University of California, Los Angeles, demonstrates the importance of Paulo Freire in the development of adult education in Latin America and the influence he has had on the international educational policies of countries such as Mexico, Cuba, and Nicaragua. Torres also points to the influence of John Dewey and Antonio Gramsci on the work of Paulo Freire, as well as the similarities between Freire's theories and those of the German philosopher Jürgen Habermas.

Torres is currently concluding what will surely prove to be one of the most significant works on Freire, *Paulo Freire: Political Philosophy of Education.* To begin with, he demonstrates the philosophies which marked the work of Freire: existentialism, phenomenology, and Marxism. Above all, he emphasizes the influence that Freire received from his readings of Hegel and Marx, with reference to, for example, the criticism of religion and theology, of philosophy and politics and social and economic alienation. The dialectic between the Master and the Slave, developed by Hegel, can be considered the principal theoretical framework of *Pedagogy of the Oppressed.* It could be said that the whole of his theory of conscientization has its roots in Hegel. It is also clear that this theory is influenced by the dialogue Freire maintained with the Brazilian philosopher Álvaro Vieira

Pinto, author of *Consciência e realidade nacional*, published in 1960, and the reading of Frantz Fanon's book *The Wretched of the Earth*, published in 1965, and Albert Memmi's book *The Colonizer and the Colonized*, published in 1967.

In press today (1992), also, is one of the most comprehensive and innovative studies of Freire's work and its implications for educators and cultural workers in the United States—*Paulo Freire: A Critical Encounter*, edited by Peter McLaren and Peter Leonard.

Paulo Freire Today

The present-day readings of Paulo Freire, an indefatigable reader, include classic and contemporary Marxist authors: Jürgen Habermas, Bogdan Suchodolski, Georges Snyders, Rosa Luxemburg, Agnes Heller, Claude Leffort, George Lukács, Louis Althusser, and E. J. Hobsbawm.

In 1983, with its Regional Program for Abandoned and Street Children, UNICEF began a series of support activities for governments, the Catholic Church, private institutions, and communities, in the search for alternative means of rescuing and helping the abandoned children of Latin America.

An initial step in this proposal was the publication in Spanish of *Paulo Freire e os educadores de rua*, which aimed at attracting attention to plight of abandoned children who were born and who live in the street, in a situation of considerable risk. In this book, Paulo Freire discusses the circumstances which produced these children, the practice of street education, its perplexities, its surprising pedagogical features, and its general characteristics. He proposes a pedagogy that, on one hand, rejects the authoritarianism that suffocates freedom, and, on the other, that rejects licentious irresponsibility

Since he returned to Brazil, Paulo Freire has taken part in many events, courses, and seminars in the most diverse institutions, always treating them as political and pedagogical acts. Together with Martin Carnoy, he gave an intensive course in the School of Education at Stanford University, California and he opened the Education Forum in the state of São Paulo, Brazil, in August 1983.

He has also received diverse homages and various titles, such as the King Balduin Prize for International Development, in Belgium, and the UNESCO 1986 Prize for Education for Peace.

When he received this last prize, Paulo Freire said: "Peace is created and constituted by overcoming perverse social realities. Peace is created and is constituted by the neverending construction of social justice. Because of this, I do not believe in any education for a peace movement which, instead of revealing the world of injustices, makes it opaque and blinds its victims."

Only in June 1987 did Paulo Freire manage to get his place back as a professor at the Federal University of Pernambuco, through a bill passed by the New Republic, which thus made up for the injustice of the military government in 1964.

At the moment, Paulo Freire is a consultant at the University of Campinas and at the Catholic University of Campinas. He also gives occasional courses at other universities.

In 1980 he joined the PT (Partido dos Trabalhadores— "the Workers' Party"), in São Paulo. From 1980 to 1986, he worked as director and founder of the Wilson Pinheiro Foundation, which was linked to the PT. He directly supervised the adult literacy project, which was organized by this foundation in the town of Diadema, in Greater São Paulo.

The account of some of his educational experiences at this time can be found in his published "dialogues" with other intellectuals and educators. He tried a new methodological paradigm in the line of the participatory research, putting into practice a theory of knowledge which has as its main dimension the dialogic nature of the production of knowledge. Paulo Freire thus contributed toward a historical understanding of scientific rigor.

He has said the following about this rigor:

Rigor, as a methodological approximation of the object which offers us decisive knowledge, is not born all of a sudden. It is forged in history and implies a practice in the intimacy of which there is always a possibility of overcoming a previous ingenuous procedure, which had been thought to be both valid and critical. The historical nature of rigor and of the exactitude of the findings, without which there can be no science, explains, on the other hand, the historicity of knowledge. What can happen is that some people feel insecure when they discover that science fails to give them a definitive knowledge and they wonder: "If it's like this, what do I do?" I believe that at the moment that this obvious statement is made, curiosity and the search for a greater rigor for more exact findings grow.[2]

The experience of Paulo Freire with this methodology is recorded in a series of works, among them, the two volumes (1984) of *Sobre a educação*, written together with Sérgio Guimarães, in which Paulo Freire examines childhood, adolescence, and school through his own childhood, adolescence, and schooling. He also studies the impact of the means of mass communication on present-day education.

As for television, he has said in dialogue with Sérgio Guimarães

> I am a man of television. I am also a man of radio. I watch soap operas, for example, and I learn a lot by criticizing them. I find this funny. As a viewer, I demand such a lot from myself that watching television programs tires me because I don't easily give in. I fight with it, if you can understand. A commercial rarely catches me unawares. Very rarely. I analyze the commercials. You could say, "But Paulo, you can't watch television in this way [he laughs] as if you were in a class." No. But this is my way of being: I make a general analysis of commercials and I immediately find in them the class, sex, and racial division, if you follow me. I already did this in Europe, where the division is much less obvious than here in Brazil.
>
> When I think about the problem of the so-called means of communication, it soon becomes clear that I feel a man of my time. I am not against television. However, I think, and I don't know if you will agree with me, that it is impossible to think about the problem of the means of communication without thinking of the problem of power. This means that the means of communication are neither good nor bad in themselves. They are the result of technical advances, expressions of human creativity, of science developed by mankind. The problem is that of knowing who and what they serve. And this is a

question that is connected to power and politics. I am convinced that when this problematic situation is resolved, the means of communication can provide us with technical solutions.[3]

On the subject of information technology, Paulo Freire has said

I am not against information technology, I'm not against the use of computers. I have already said that this is part of my being a man of my time. The problem is that of knowing who and what will be served if information technology begins to play a large part in Brazilian education . . . .What is behind this? Quite definitely it is an experience of class. My worry is that the introduction of these more sophisticated means into the educational field will, once more, work in favor of those who have and against those who have not. It is because of this that I say that the criticism is not a technical criticism but a political one.[9]

Together with Frei Betto (1985), in *Essa escola chamada vida*, he takes another look at the theme of the exercise of reflection together with practice as the best way of learning: both learn lessons from exile and from prison.

Together with Antonio Faundez (1985), a Chilean philosopher, he wrote *Learning to Question: A Pedagogy of Liberation*, a dialogue in which he analyzes the role of the intellectual in societies in transformation, like that of Allende's Chile and those of Guinea-Bissau and Nicaragua. He makes two important observations about literacy schemes in Africa. Any scheme will fail unless it takes into account the deeply rooted traditions of oral communication, which can give problems to the literacy process. Paulo Freire also had problems developing his ideas there because of another characteristic which is often found in Africa, as an inheritance of colonialism: the authoritarianism.

Together with myself and Sérgio Guimarães (1985), reflecting on our work both in Brazil and abroad, in *Pedagogia: diálogo e conflito*, he replies to some of the questions that are most frequently asked us, focusing on them from the angle of the pedagogy of dialogue and the pedagogy of conflict. This book concentrates above all on the problems of knowledge, power, and education.

The central idea of this book is that the pedagogy of dialogue does not exclude the notion of conflict. On the contrary, the philosophy of dialogue values conflict and works to overcome it. It considers conflict legitimate and relies on it as a means of fully realizing authentic dialogue. Conflict is the engine of history. The nature of society and knowledge develop as a result of the unity and opposition of opposing forces. This is why conflictive relationships can be viewed in a positive light. *Pedagogy of conflict* shows a love for freedom, commitment, and clarity of purpose. It is therefore both personal and existential, human and social.

What then is the difference between the pedagogy of conflict which we advocate and Freire's pedagogy of dialogue?

This difference was the central issue around which we "dialogued" in this book. We concluded that it was a matter of emphasis on one or the other category (dialogue or conflict). Dialogue, not consensus, is imperative in dealing with conflict. Dialogue within conflict works toward overcoming and integrating without eliminating the opposition. Pedagogy of conflict is essentially dialectical. It is placed in a dialectical integrative view of education. As such, it can be considered much more as an open view of education than as a closed position which works to exclude other tendencies.

Together with the North American educator Ira Shor (1987), Paulo Freire wrote *Medo e ousadia: o cotidiano do professor*. This book examines the daily work of the teacher, which is the source of numerous contradictions and conflicts. The very different experiences of the authors are connected by the same focus, that of liberating education and by a similar dream of a society of equality. Both are especially interested in what they call *empowerment*, the creative and dynamic possibilities of education as a means of change.

Aprendendo com a própria história, written together with Sérgio Guimarães, is still incomplete. The first volume came out in 1987. This work is an autobiographical account of his own journey, of the turning points in his life as an intellectual and as an educator.

Following the same line as their previous publications, in 1987 Paulo Freire and Donaldo Macedo published *Literacy: Reading the Word and the World*, in which they examine the present crisis of alphabetization.[5]

In recent years, Paulo Freire's thinking has been influential in the Unites States, through dialogues with important educators such as Jonathan Kozol, Martin Carnoy, Carlos Alberto Torres, Stanley Aronowitz, Michael W. Apple, Donaldo Macedo, Ira Shor, Peter McLaren, Henry A. Giroux, and others.

In December 1990 a new book by Paulo Freire was published, written together with the North American educator Myles Horton—*We Make the Road by Walking: Conversations on Education and Social Change*. It is a book written with a great deal of passion, hope, and wisdom. Both authors have been educators and political activists. Myles Horton (1905–90) was the founder of Highlander Center, in the South of the United States, which played an enormously important role in the civil-rights movement and the education of young people and workers during the fifties and sixties. The life and work of Horton greatly resemble those of Paulo Freire. Despite following different paths, they came together to discuss their respective experiences and ideas, and found many similarities in their views and methods of working.

Freire's books in dialogue form can be considered a form of Cartesian meditation, as Carlos Alberto Torres told me, on the practice of education and the everyday reality of the educator. Although Freire deals with scientific themes, the style of these recent books is much more literary than that of his first books.

Why did Paulo Freire begin to work in this manner? It is clear that various explanations are possible, but one in particular seems to me to be the most relevant: Paulo Freire is a native of the Northeast of Brazil, which has a strong oral tradition. He is known to be a great teller of stories. With these books in dialogue form Freire has compared his thinking to other thinkers and has also related it to the totality of sciences, from the humanities to the natural and applied sciences. These works have also contributed to the extension of his pedagogy, beyond education to other areas of knowledge. Perhaps he has been working toward the realization of one of Gramsci's greatest aims:

> To create a new culture does not signify merely to make individual "original" discoveries; it signifies as well, and above all, to critically disseminate truths

already discovered, to socialize them; to transform them; however this should be based upon vital actions, within the coordination of intellectual and moral order. The fact that a multitude of men can be made to think about the present reality, coherently and in a united manner is a "philisophical" fact of much more importance and originality than a discovery, by a philosophical "genius," of a new truth which remains the patrimony of a small group of intellectuals.[6]

At the age of seventy-one, known throughout the world as the greatest educator of our time, Paulo Freire lost his wife, which hurt him tremendously. We could imagine that there wouldn't be anything left for him to do. But this didn't happen. After spending some months in pain, struggling not to get depressed, Paulo Freire began again to slowly involve himself with education and with change.

Paulo Freire returned to producing intensively. He is renewing himself and he says that he would like to live everything again. Fate took him again to Pernambuco, where, accepting an offer by Miguel Arraes, once more State Governor, he became a consultant to the Department of Education. He accepted the challenge of helping to reformulate education in the state he was born in.

Elza's death left him with two paths: dying with her or choosing life. The choice for life incorporated Elza with optimistic memories, because at her side there was also the option for revolution.

6

A Revolutionary Educator

In his process of self-criticism, which is coherent with the principle of not dichotomizing practice and theory, Paulo Freire has admitted on a number of occasions that he has found himself nagged by subjectivism. This fact resulted in his giving up using the term *conscientization* some years ago. This concept has frequently been thought of as a pure taking of conscience of reality, without the necessary action to transform it. For Paulo Freire, this conscientization passes, first and foremost, through the practice, through the transforming action. Even so, in order to avoid subjectivist interpretations, he abandoned the concept.

Coherence: Theory and Practice

Paulo Freire has said that he made a number of ingenuous errors in the years before 1964 as a result of an atmosphere of intense popular participation. This political climate gave rise to a kind of magical vision of the word, of discourse. The more powerful were slogans like "land reform by law or by force" and "the process cannot be reversed," the better. It was as if it was enough merely to reveal the oppressive reality in order to achieve liberation from the oppressors. "I believe that the atmosphere also deceived us, as the amount of ideology and politics increased without corresponding changes in infrastructure." In his first book, Paulo Freire admits that he himself fell into the trap of this kind of idealism.

As for the present situation, Paulo Freire says,

> My suggestion is that we believe less in the mythification and the magic of the word. It is not strong discourse that is important. Let's work more and speak less. Let us give ourselves to a task of popular organization and mobilization. This is not done through vehement speeches but through a well thought-out practice, about which one can readily reflect critically.[1]

In the fifteen years I have been working with Paulo Freire, what I have most noticed has been his practice of a category which is fundamental to his pedagogy. This is his coherence, which is connected to other categories, for example, his radicalism and historical patience.

This coherence between the educationalist and the man is not just something he has written about but is part of his way of being and can be seen in the smallest details of his life, whenever and wherever he may be. Paulo Freire always pays attention; he is always analyzing his practice and the concrete action around him. As a teacher, he always analyzes at length what a student says. And when he doesn't agree, he doesn't answer aggressively but strongly defends his points of view. This shows his respect for his interlocutor.

But this respect doesn't make him lose his attention. Autonomy doesn't mean abandonment, laissez-faire. He always intervenes, he never stays out of the discussion, and he constantly gives his opinion. In this he is directive. As a teacher, Freire has always been the director of the process of learning, using the information that has sedimented through his considerable experience.

He behaves in the same way outside the classroom. On one occasion we were invited to lunch by a publishing company to discuss the publication of a book. When the executive of the publishing company paid the bill and asked for a receipt, the waiter asked him: "For the same value?" The executive said yes, and this made the waiter somewhat embarrassed. Paulo didn't miss the opportunity to make a comment on this dialogue, behind which one could see the whole game of corruption. The executive could have asked for a receipt with a higher value and pocketed the difference, which is common. The waiter, aware of this, asked the value before making out the receipt.

Paulo is not moralistic. If being moralistic could bring about the revolution, he wouldn't have the slightest hesitation in being so. But he immediately adds, "This is not the way to finish with capitalism."

In 1985, when the National Congress passed a bill that would give the vote to illiterates, television wanted to know Paulo Freire's opinion. In the course of a quick interview, the reporter asked the following question: "So are we now going to teach illiterates how to vote?" I remember that Paulo put his arm on the shoulder of the reporter and said: "It's not quite like that. They'll soon learn how to vote. They just need to vote." And he added, "The dominant class would like to teach the people to vote in their way. And it's this that they must be thinking of doing now to control the illiterates' votes."

The following year, elections took place. However, few illiterates turned out to vote. Having been manipulated for many years by paternalistic and corrupt politicians, the popular masses didn't believe that they could change anything through voting.

Paulo Freire, an educator who has been struggling through at least four decades for the education of those who are learning literacy and whose help has been requested by governments, liberation armies, religious institutions, and so forth, knows that just voting is not enough. A citizen who takes part not just on election day must be made.

No Reply Is Definitive

Paulo Freire criticizes the critics who fail to understand his ideas and their historical circumstances. For the same reason, he criticizes those of his followers who take his theories word for word, outside their context. He even criticizes them for just being content with his first texts and not reading the critiiques he has made on his own work through the course of his written work, showing that learning and relearning never end.

When Paulo Freire is asked to speak, he normally asks the audience to begin the session with their own questions. In general, after some moments of silence, someone raises a question. When no one says anything, he begins his talk or asks for a piece of candy or a chocolate to clear his throat. He thus makes the atmosphere pleasant, prepares the ground for the points he will make, and, while he is eating the candy, he begins the dialogue, often with the other members of the panel. He likes to speak "with someone else." One one occasion, in Denmark, he spoke for almost four hours to an audience of approximately a thousand teachers and students, trying to link various types of thinking and trends of contemporary education. It is easy to talk about what you are doing, what you do, willingly, joyfully, lovingly.

Another time, the first question that was asked him was, "What is questioning?" He worked on this worrying question and showed that the act of questioning is tied to the act of existing, of being, of studying, of building, of researching, of knowing. He talked about the validity of all kinds of questions and stated, "No reply is definitive." Because of this, we should always continue to question, as asking is the essence of the act of knowing. He also said that authoritarian teachers very often end up by repressing their pupils' questions or reply to questions that the pupils don't make. Therefore, all authoritarian teachers are dull, uninteresting, and treat their pupils as if they didn't exist. By acting like this, they will only manage to suffocate the pleasure of asking, researching, and knowing.

Paulo took this question—"What is questioning?"—home. It marked him, followed him , and later inspired the dense work, *Por uma pedagogia da pergunta*, which he wrote together with Antonio Faundez.

Coherence, which he defends as the first virtue of the revolutionary educator, is his main virtue. But he frequently warns us that total coherence is stupidity, since it makes people incapable of changing. In order to change, one must disrespect the truths which one has already acquired, one's own prejudices.

Absolute coherence would be the negation of history and the negation of the fact that man makes history through his own history. The coherence of him who speaks is the coherence between the discourse that announces the politico-pedagogical choice and the practice that should be at the service of this announcement, confirming the discourse.

Coherence is not a scientific or a subjectivist attitude of mind; it is a theoretical conception of the educational act, one of the fundamental categories of the theory of liberating education and popular education. This dialogic theory is opposed to the antidialogic theory of the dominant class. Because of this, Paulo Freire cannot accept the position of those who want to "free others while they are dominators"; in other words, the position of those who call themselves revolutionaries but continue to use the authoritarian methods of the dominant class. He has denounced false revolutionaries, those who want to make the revolution alone as they have no confidence in the popular masses. He finds this incoherent. Liberation is not the work of one person, one group or one party; it's the work of everyone.

In the preface to the book written by Henry Giroux, *Radical Pedagogy*, Freire insists that the revolutionary educator must be coherent. It is frequently necessary to pay a heavy price for coherence between what one does, says, and writes. The coherence of an educator is not limited just to teaching. He gives an example of incoherence: the educator who, considering all politico-pedagogical action ingenuous that comes from the comprehension that popular groups have of their concrete situation says that he is not elitist.

The Revolutionary Educator: Patiently Impatient

However, coherence should be seen within a dialectic vision, and not metaphysically. It is an incoherent coherence since, as Paulo Freire often says, the revolutionary must be patiently impatient to be able to distinguish the ideal from the possible. The revolutionary only does the possible today, but, as he is impatiently patient, tomorrow he will do what today is impossible.

If one loses this dialectic principle, one may find oneself in the spontaneous posture of someone who folds his arms, hoping that history is made mechanically, or alternatively in the authoritarian posture of someone who has lost his historical patience and acts as if history depended on himself and on his thinking alone. This principle can be translated into practice by what he calls "democratic radicalism," which is neither social democracy or reformism. For Paulo Freire, democratic radicalism is a synonym of the revolution which is possible, and of socialism.

What does being patient and impatient at the same time mean? It means that one must accept the fact that one is situated at a definite historical moment. Breaking with the historical moment can mean two things: it is either broken through patience or through impatience. The first is the case with the voluntarists, those who lose historical patience and believe that theory can change history regardless of the circumstances. As Paulo Freire has said, the voluntarists want to "make the revolution by Thursday."

The second case in point is that of the immobilists, the mechanists, those who break with impatience in favor of an unlimited patience. They end up in passivity, in grassrootism, (the act of leaving the responsibility in the hands of the grassroots and leaving themselves out), in spontaneity, which is another way of denying history. Paulo Freire therefore says that the revolutionary educator should be patiently impatient, by keeping a dynamic relationship between patience and impatience. He has frequently remarked on this virtue in Amílcar Cabral, the author of this expression.

Pedagogy of Indignation

At a teachers' congress in Goiânia, Brazil, soon after returning from exile, Paulo Freire spent nearly forty

FIGURE 8

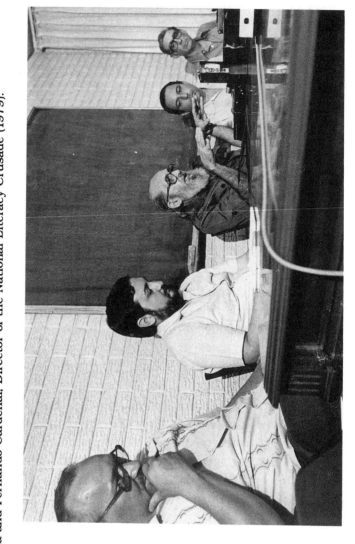

Paulo Freire in Manágua, with Hugo Asmann, Arturo Ornelas, Carlos Tunnermann, Minister of Education of Nicaragua and Fernando Cardenal, Director of the National Literacy Crusade (1979).

minutes reading a sermon by Antônio Vieira, in which he said that none of Christ's miracles took as long as it would to cure a mute who had been visited by the devil. This would have given Christ a lot of work. Paulo Freire, who was speaking about authoritarianism in Brazilian education, added that this has been the great illness in Brazil: the silence which the people had submitted to. What Vieira didn't say, because, at that time, he couldn't make an analysis of social classes, is that, above all in Brazil, those who have been mute are the popular classes, the working classes. This mutism doesn't mean that the popular classes don't do anything or that they stop rebelling. There is a history of rebellion in Brazil which the official history doesn't tell or makes a point of forgetting.

Against this authoritarianism of the elites, including the intellectual elites, he proposes speech, the shout, as the pedagogy of the oppressed.

It must be pointed out that there is no incoherence between the pedagogy of the dialogue and the pedagogy of indignation, between dialogue and violence. The pedagogy of the oppressed looks forward to peace, but it doesn't refuse to fight for it. This is a recurring theme in Paulo Freire's work. It is violence that imposes the situation of domination/oppression. According to Freire, violence prevents man from being. The dominant class and above all the means of communication inculcate the idea that the popular classes, called marginals, are violent, without noticing that the dominant classes themselves instigate this violence throught the exploitation of labor.

Already in *Pedagogy of the Oppressed*, Paulo Freire insisted on the fact that violence is not instigated by the oppressed:

How could the oppressed begin violence if they are the result of such violence? How could they be the initiators of something, which, on being objectively instigated, constructs them? There would be no oppressed if there were no relationship of violence which made them conform as violated people, in an objective situation of oppression. It is those who oppress, those who exploit, those who don't recognize themselves in others who inaugurate the violence; it is not the oppressed, the exploited, who are not recognized by those who exploit as others. Those who introduce lack of love are not those who are not loved but those who do not love. Those who introduce fear are not the weak, w ohare subjected to it, but the violent ones, who, with their power, create the concrete situation which creates those who have been "rejected from life," the ragged. It is not the tyrannized but the tyrants who introduce tyranny. It is not the hated but those who first hate that introduce hatred. It is not those who had their humanity denied who introduce the denial of men but those who denied their humanity, and in so doing they deny their own humanity. It is not those who become weak under the force of the powerful who introduce force, but the powerful who weaken them.[2]

Paulo Freire has reaffirmed this position throughout his life. In 1982, fourteen years after *Pedagogy of the Oppressed*, he takes up the same thesis: "It is not the unloved who introduce lack of love but those who don't love." He also talks about the relationship between violence and the class struggle.

If you wish, take out the words "class struggle," which are overused, and say "class conflict, conflict of interests." This exists. And it wasn't even Marx who invented this. He himself said, in one of his letters, that the bourgeois economists had written about the class struggle before him. As an educator, I can't deny or flee the conflicts. It is impossible to deny the conflicts. And I would add that conflict gives birth to conscience. My dream—and I think it's possible—is the following: to find the paths which lead to social transformation with less wastage. The less social expense, the better. But I can understand the existence of conflict and struggle, and conflict can even be generative.[3]

In recent years, Paulo Freire has added two other categories to those I have mentioned: indignation and invasion.

By considering the limits that have been imposed by the historical circumstances, not only for educators, he has demanded the right for the educator to become indignant. He believes that the pedagogy of indignation is necessary to the revolutionary educator in this oppressive society. This Paulo Freire is at the service of the popular classes and against the bourgeois order. He thus recommends that popular educators, when they occupy the space that the apparatus of the school that the state provides for them, occupy it not as faithful servants but as invaders of the bourgeois state.

It is within this conception that Paulo Freire defends the popular public school. He has repeated on many occasions that what he most noticed when he returned from exile was the spectacle of big business connected with education, which had been the result of a policy of privatization which had been encouraged by the dictatorship. This, he said, existed on a much smaller scale before the coup of 1964.

As far as a proposal for education in Brazil which is coherent with his positions is concerned, Paulo Freire has said that education in a country should not be decided by one person alone, but rather by a group, by many teams, by the people.[4] He said that if he took part in one of these teams, he would do everything possible to find ways through which public schools could overcome three basic situations: the contradiction between theory and practice; the contradiction between manual and intellectual work; the dichotomy between previous and new knowledge; in other words, not dichotomizing, for example, research and teaching.

The "Last" Freire

The Spanish educator Antonio Monclús has called the period of Paulo Freire's books which are written in dialogue the phase of the "last" Freire. In his work *Pedagogía de la contradicción: Paulo Freire*, he tries to show that Paulo Freire's texts are not limited just to the world of education but that they are also a reference point for the theoretical analysis and practice of another great present-day worry in Latin America, the search for a Latin American identity.

When we talk of the "latter" Paulo Freire, we can see a definite trajectory along which he develops a way of teaching and creates a language. In this evolution we can see some thematic differences between the classic works of Paulo Freire, which have been in print for two decades, like *Pedagogy of the Oppressed*, and the present-day works.

What has happened along this trajectory?

Firstly, the balance between Christian and Marxist themes has been broken, and greater emphasis is found in his recent works on social themes. He therefore reflects less on the action of the church. But Paulo Freire still emphasizes his position in favor of a church that is committed not just to conscientization, but also to the political organization of the popular classes.

Secondly, through his contact with the Brazilian situation after his return from exile, Paulo Freire has been very concerned with the problem of the public school and formal education. This theme is not new in Paulo Freire, but it was inevitable that he went deeper into it in his frequent meetings with Brazilian educators, who are worried about the universalization of basic education and the position of the public school. Paulo Freire's contribution to present-day Brazilian educational thinking is very much associated with his experience, which has been connected to a popular public school.

Monclús thus notes some differences between the first and the present-day Paulo Freire. His cultural action in adult literacy continues although one can find at the moment a reinvention of his work, something new, in the public schools, especially in municipal schools.

It is possible that Paulo Freire, a man of his time, is now involved in something which is bigger than him; the change of the social function of the public school, moving towards a popular and socialist public school. This school is slowly being born inside the capitalist public school.

So-called popular education, which takes place outside state organs or against it, has undoubtedly reached a crisis point in recent years. With the exception of groups connected to the church and the so-called community schools, there are few institutions that can offer a formal popular education. Those which do exist are often connected to syndicates. What the popular segments of society would really like are quality public schools at all levels and grades, for children, young people, and adults. "Education is the duty of the state and the right of everyone" can be heard throughout Brazil.

In view of these historical circumstances, Paulo Freire has insisted on the necessity of transforming public schools, which are now under the control of the state bureaucracy. Therefore, the population must win the right to this kind of school through mechanisms of popular control such as popular councils. This was the position that Paulo Freire took to the Constituent Assembly on May 18th, 1987, when, together with myself, he made a statement to the Subcommission on Education, Culture and Sport, saying that the defense of the public school was a "vital struggle," the "fundamental struggle" of Brazilian educators in the new Constitution.[5]

Paulo Freire as Public Administrator

Paulo Freire was able to put his ideas into practice as Secretary of Education from 1989 to 1991 in São Paulo, Brazil's largest city, with a population of twelve million.

On November 15, 1988, the PT (Workers' Party) won the municipal elections in São Paulo. Paulo Freire was nominated as Secretary of Education and took up the position on January, 1, 1989. For the first time, a popular party would take power, in the most important economic and political city in the country, with Luiza Erundina, a social worker and teacher of social administration, as mayor.

For those who knew Paulo Freire well, his administrative ability came as no surprise.[6] His secret was to know how to govern democratically. In nearly two years as head of the Municipal Secretariat of Education, he was able to set up a team of five to six advisors who were

FIGURE 9

Paulo Freire in 1989 as Municipal Secretary of Education at a
demonstration against censorship of books in schools in the
previous municipal administration. He is beside Luíza Erundina,
Mayoners of São Paulo, and Frei Betto.

allowed to work with great autonomy and could substitute
for him without any problems of continuity in his policies.
A single weekly meeting took place in which general
policy guidelines and decisions of actions taken were
discussed. If necessary, a new or different course was
taken. Paulo Freire would ardently defend his opinions,
though he knew how to work in a team, contradicting the
spontaneism of which he was so often accused. He had
authority but exercised it democratically and confronted
difficult situations with considerable patience. He would
say that the work of change in education demanded
historical patience because education is a long-term
process.

He found a Secretariat pedagogically empty and physically in ruin. He stated in February 1989 to the São Paulo magazine *Leia*:

If we not only construct more classrooms, but also zealously keep them clean, joyful, and beautiful, sooner or later the very beauty of the space will require yet another beauty: that of competence in teaching, the joy of learning, the creative imagination, with the freedom to exercise itself, the adventure of creating.[7]

What are the most important structural changes introduced in the municipal school system by Freire's administration?

He himself replies in a book on his experience as the head of the Secretariat: "The most important structural changes introduced in the school took place with respect to the autonomy of the school.[8] School councils and student unions were created. In the same vein, Freire continues: "The greatest advance at the level of school autonomy was to permit from within the heart of the school the generation of each school's own pedagogical project which, with administrative support, can accelerate the transformation of the school.[9]

To illustrate that process of change I will present three examples: the program for permanent training; the program for the literacy training of young people and adults; and the practice of an interdisciplinary curriculum.

1. The Program for Permanent Training

From the begining of this administration, Paulo Freire insisted that he was deeply committed to the permanent formation of the municipal educators. His program of teacher training was oriented by the following principles and fundamental tenets.[10]

Principles:

a. The educator is the subject of his/her practice; the creation and recreation of an educational action through a reflection upon his/her everyday practice is his/her responsibility.
b. The training of the educator should be permanent and systematized, because the practice is formulated and reformulated.
c. Pedagogical practice requires the comprehension of the very genesis of knowledge, in other words, how the process of knowing takes place.
d. The program of training educators is a precondition for the process of reorientation of the curriculum in schools.

Fundamental tenets:

a. The physiognomy of the envisaged school is as important as the horizon of the pedagogical proposal.
b. The need to offer basic training for educators in the different subject areas.
c. The appropriation, on the part of educators, of the scientific advances of human knowledge, envisaged with the possibility of contributing to the school.

With this program, Paulo Freire intended to train teachers for a new pedagogical posture, considering, above all, Brazil's five-hundred-year authoritarian tradition. Such an entrenched tradition cannot be overcome in just a few years. Paulo Freire battled successfully against this tradition with political decisiveness, technical competence, love, and, above all, the exercise of democracy.

The training of the educator transcends simple theoretical courses on democracy. Training take place through practice and authentic participation of teachers in a democratic process. The practice of democracy is of much more value than a course on democracy.

2. The Literacy Program for Young People and Adults

Luiza Erundina had been elected to govern the largest city in South America, with a clear proposal to invert priorities. Her election opened up better possibilities for introducing popular participation.

To make possible the democratization of decisions it was necessary: (1) to respect the autonomy of social movements and their organization; (2) to open channels for participation, starting from the new administration; and (3) administrative transparency, that is, broad democratization of information.

Popular participation is an effective process of adult education, for it develops and strengthens the population's awareness of citizenship in order to take on their role of subjects in transforming the city. The most important theory is that the population—organized or not—has a basic idea of how the administration works, how the budget is made and how the laws which determine public administration and also limit the transforming action are worked out. Effective popular participation without democratizing information is not possible.

Based on these political and pedagogical preconditions, the Secretariat of Education set up a literacy program for young people and adults entitled MOVA-SP

(Literacy Movement in the City of São Paulo). MOVA-SP, which is based on the work of Paulo Freire and another popular educator, Pedro Pontual, has been put into action.

Since the begining of 1989, representatives of popular movements already working in adult literacy have consulted the Secretariat to see what kind of support they could get from the municipal administration in order to extend their work.

In April of the same year, a symposium was held where the Forum of the Popular Movements for Adult Literacy in the City of São Paulo was set up.

Through agreements with the member groups of the Forum, the Secretariat of Education has provided financial and technical resources. It is the Forum's task to define— together with the Secretariat—the criteria of the agreements through which partners take on the responsibility of setting up literacy nuclei, renting classrooms, providing didactic material, and remunerating educators and supervisors.

This project, which was inaugurated in January 1990, has had great effect both in the city of São Paulo and in other states and municipalities, due to its proposal of strengthening popular movements without attaching them to the state. It's one of the few examples of partnership between civil society and the state. Obviously, the relationship is not always harmonious. However, this is the necessary condition for the joint venture between the state and the popular movements.

MOVA-SP doen't impose a single methodological orientation or, as people always say, "Paulo Freire's method." The intention is to maintain pluralism. Only pedagogical methods which are antiscientific and belong to authoritarian or racist philosophies are not accepted.

Even without imposing any methodology, MOVA-SP keeps its political and pedagogical principles.[11] These can

FIGURE 10

Paulo Freire as Municipal Secretary of Education, with the coordinating team of the 1st Congress of Adult Literacy Students of MOVA-SP, in the City of São Paulo, in 1990.

be summarized in the idea of a liberating conception of education. This contains the following elements: the role of education in constructing a new historical project; our theory of knowledge which is based on concrete production in constructing knowledge; and comprehension of literacy not just as a logical and intellectual process but also as one that is deeply affective and social.

In order to make a literacy movement into a collective effort, experience must be the main source of knowledge. Otherwise, it will be reduced to mere intellectual knowledge which doesn't lead to critical awareness and to strengthening popular power, that is, creating and developing popular organizations.

What is being developed must not be confused with literacy campaigns. Failures experienced in many literacy campaigns in Latin America and especially in Brazil, made us avoid even the word *campaign*. We want to stress the character of continuity and permanence of the movement we want to construct.

What is most important today for idealizers of MOVA-SP and the popular movements which support it is that the work will be continued as an integrated part of the city's education system.

MOVA-SP is part of a strategy of cultural action directed toward recovering citizenship: to train leaders, to make people intellectually more autonomous, to prepare multipliers of liberating social action. MOVA-SP has contributed to strengthening popular social movements and to establishing new alliances between civil society and the state.[12]

3. The Practice of Constructing an Interdisciplinary Curriculum

The extensiveness of Paulo Freire's work and his numerous passages through various areas of knowledge and practice takes us to another central theme in his work: interdisciplinarity.

In 1987 and 1988, Paulo Freire developed the concept of interdisciplinarity in dialogues with educators from various fields in the University of Campinas, who were committed to a project for popular informal education. The concept of interdisciplinarity evolves from the analysis of concrete practice and of lived experience of the "reflection group." The reflections made by this university group were organized and published by Débora Mazza and Adriano Nogueira in *Fazend escola conhecendo a vida,* 1986. The following year, as Secretary of Education, Paulo Freire started an important movement for the changes in the curriculum. This would be called the "projeto de interdisciplinaridade" (the project for interdisciplinarity or project "Inter").

Pedagogical action through interdisciplinarity and transdisciplinarity points towards the construction of a school which participates in the formation of the social agent. The educator, subject of his pedagogical action, is able to elaborate programs and methods of teaching and learning, gaining competence in the effort to insert the school in the community. The fundamental objective of interdisciplinarity is to live the experience of a global reality that takes place within the everyday life of the students, teachers, and the community. In the traditional school this experience is compartmentalized and fragmented. Joining wisdom, knowledge, firsthand experience, school, community, environment, and so forth, is the objective of interdisciplinarity, which develops into a practice of collective joint work in the organization of the school. There is no interdisciplinarity without decentralization of power, and no decentralization, without an effective autonomy of the school.[13]

Paulo Freire left the Municipal Secretariat of Education on May 27th, 1991. After almost two and a half years, he returned to his library and academic activities in "the manner of he who, despite leaving, remains," as he affirms in the epilogue of his book *A educação na cidade.*[14]

In fact Paulo Freire has continued as an active presence in the Secretariat, offering his extensive experience to help the Secretariat's project. He states in his farewell address: "Even though I no longer am Secretary, I will continue at your side in a different form . . . .You can continue to count on me in the construction of an educational policy for a school with a new 'face,' more joyful, fraternal, and democratic."[15]

7

Paulo Freire in the Context of Contemporary Pedagogical Thought

The thinking of Paulo Freire can be related to that of many contemporary educators. He has been compared to Pichon-Rivière, a psychologist who was born in Geneva and who moved at a very early age to the Argentinian Chaco. Pichon-Rivère's experience of two very different cultures opened his thinking, made it nonethnocentric and nonauthoritarian; and although he and Paulo Freire follow two different practices, both have something in common: they look for transformation through critical conscience.

Paulo Freire's focus has also been compared to that of the North American educator Theodore Brameld. Both emphasize the dialogue between educator and pupil, the relationship between politics and education, and the acquisition of knowledge as a social factor.

Recently, a parallel was made between the work of Paulo Freire and that of Enrique Dussel, one of the theoreticians of liberation theology.[1]

Another comparison is with the Polish educator, Janusz Korczak (1878–1942), who died together with two hundred pupils in a nazi gas chamber. He became a legendary example of a pedagogy which was centered in love, self-management, and anti-authoritarianism.

After having received an honorary doctorate in Educational Sciences from the University of Geneva in 1979, Paulo Freire was compared to Eduard Claparède, the founder of the famous Institut Jean-Jacques Rousseau of Educational Sciences in 1912. He was also compared to Pierre Bovet, who like the other educationalists mentioned, believed in the political role of education for peace.

We can also find a great affinity between Paulo Freire and the revolutionary French educator, Célestin Freinet (1896–1966)[2] in the way that both believe that the pupil can organize his own learning. Freinet gave enormous importance to what he called the "free text." Like Paulo Freire, he used the so-called global method of alphabetization, associating the reading of the word with the reading of the world. He insisted on the necessity, both for children and adults, of understanding the text when reading it. Like Paulo Freire, he worried about the education of the popular classes. His work method included printing, free drawing, dialogue, and contact with the reality of the pupil.

Lígia Chiappini Moraes Leite sees a great similarlty between the work of Paulo Freire and that of Freinet, especially in what is referred to as the role of the imagination and creativity in the child's developmental process. She also draws a parallel with Gramsci's idea of the militant educator.

Lígia Chiappini also sees Rousseau[3] as a source of inspiration for Paulo Freire, particularly when Rousseau says that he would be at the side of Émile (his imaginary pupil) when he would learn a profession as, in the words of Rousseau, "I am sure he will only learn what we learn together."

There are those, like Wilson de Faria, who say that Paulo Freire follows the tradition of pragmatism in education, in the way that he "rejects verbalism and emphasizes the value of scientific method."

Paulo Freire has kept up correspondence and friendship with Bogdan Suchodolski, one of the best-known contemporary Marxist educators, author of the well-known treatise, *A Marxist Theory of Education*. Freire considers him to be one of the greatest present-day humanists and has frequently called him "the last of the great humanists."

Madan Sarup, British sociologist, believes that the new European sociologists have been considerably influenced by Paulo Freire although Paulo Freire himself has never said that he has any connection with sociology. His thinking has undermined the traditional hierarchies, especially the pupil-teacher relationship.

In this chapter, we shall analyze four authors in greater detail: Carl Rogers (1902–87), author of *On Becoming a Person*, Ivan Illich (born in 1926), author of *Deschooling Society*, John Dewey (1859–1952), and Lev Vygotsky (1896–1934).

Carl Rogers and Student-Centered Learning

Although Paulo Freire doesn't defend the principle of nondirectivity in education as does the psychotherapist Carl Rogers,[4] there is no doubt that there are many points in common in the pedagogies they defend, especially in what concerns freedom of individual expression. They both believe that men themselves can solve their problems, as long as they are motivated to do so.

For both Rogers and Freire, the responsibility for education is in the hands of the pupil himself. It is the student who has the possibilities of growth and self-evaluation. Education should be centered on him instead of being centered on the teacher or on the teaching; the pupil should be the master of his own learning. In the class, knowledge should not be thrown at the pupil, nor are tests and exams ways of checking whether the learning has stayed in the child's head or whether the pupil has kept the knowledge in the way that the teacher has taught him. Education should have a vision of the pupil as a complete person, who has feelings and emotions.

Similarly to Paulo Freire's method, which tries to draw the traditionally distant figure of the teacher closer, the Rogerian approach, centered on the person, brings the relationship between patient and therapist closer, instead of maintaining the distance defended by traditional psychology.

Carl Rogers, when replying to criticism that his thinking has only been used by the middle classes, as it is politically moderate and has no meaning for the oppressed classes, developed ideas similar to those of Paulo Freire. A discussion can be found in chapter 6 of Rogers's *On Personal Power* (1977).

Paulo Freire wrote *Pedagogy of the Oppressed* in 1968, and Rogers wrote *Freedom to Learn* in 1969. The first is directed to rural workers and the second to students. There are no signs, however, that at the time of their publication, they had heard of each other's works.

Confrontation with Ivan Illich

The paths of Ivan Illich[5] and Paulo Freire have crossed on various occasions. Educational thinking in the seventies was greatly influenced by both of them.

In his book *Aprendendo com a própria história*, Paulo Freire says that he met Illich in 1962, when Ivan Illich extended one of the trips he made to Rio de Janeiro to Recife. On this occasion he received a piece of advice:

"One day you might be better known than you are today. I think that within ten years your ideas will have entered a number of places in the world. I'd like to suggest something to you: on the one hand, don't let the fame you'll probably have run to your head. Secondly, be happy when this fame has ended. Accepting that you are no longer famous is the only way to continue life." Paulo Freire added that it wasn't just this piece of advice from Illich that saved him from "silly vanities." His own practice demanded that he establish limits to these vanities.

What is there in common between Paulo Freire and Ivan Illich?

FIGURE 11

Paulo Freire beside Ivan Illich in Geneva, 1971.

In both we find a critique of the traditional school. Amidst the bureaucratization of the present-day scholastic institution, both demand that educators look to individual development and collective liberation by combating alienation at school and proposing the rediscovery of a creative autonomy. But in spite of these common points, there are some considerable differences.

In the work of Ivan Illich, one can find pessimism in relation to school as he doesn't believe that the traditional school has any future. For this reason, it will be necessary to combat school, "destroying" it, "deschooling" society. He defends, on the other hand, the noninstitutionalization of knowledge, leaving the task of learning to the individual through networks of people who would make contact with each other in accordance with their personal needs. The potential user would choose the activity he was interested in studying, and a computer would give him names of specialists in the subject. This proposal, however, would only be possible after a basic schooling.

On the other hand, in Freire we find optimism. School can change and be changed as it plays an important role in the transformation of society. The first step for this is conscientization, and, as a consequence, the education of the educator is of vital importance.

Neither has an easy remedy to solve the present crisis of educational institutions. They both propose criticism as a liberating instrument. The school of the future—or the end of school— will also be the collective fruit of the critiques of today.

We can find three main themes in Illich's thinking: (1) the church, which he belonged to as a priest; (2) school, the "sacred cow," with its dogmas and myths; and (3) industrial society, with its myths of umlimited growth and progress. In his opinion, (1) the church continues to be inquisitorial; (2) the majority of people acquire a great part of their knowledge outside school; and (3) industrial progress destroys the quality of life of contemporary man. Illich believes that school creates artificial necessities in order for it to be able to attend them and to continue existing. He criticizes the specialists in education who propose a lifelong continuous educational program. This seems to him to be a pretext to secure the "school industry" and guarantee it a growing "market" and a "clientele."

On the other hand, Paulo Freire thinks that inside the church there is a class struggle and believes in the prophetic church of the oppressed. He thinks that social revolution should take into account popular religious feeling. He is optimistic in relation to school, defending the popular public school, an institution to which everyone should have a right. He doesn't reject economic development but does reject the inequality of access to its benefits.

What brings Illich and Paulo Freire together is their profound belief in the need to make a revolution in the content and in the pedagogy of the present-day school. They both defend humanism, respect for the freedom of expression, and the freedom of organization in society. Both believe that this change is both pedagogical and political, and that the critique of the school is part of a wider critique of all contemporary civilization. Not accepting rigid schemes, they propose a wider discussion around the themes of what knowledge, education, power, and democracy are. For this they both, especially Paulo Freire, take advantage of a Marxist analysis without being sectarian. Both are often compared to pilgrims, who, amongst the complicated roads and detours of today, point out the obvious and fundamental.

Paulo Freire has the highest admiration for Illich and has repeated many times that he will still be read a lot. He has also said that Illich's analyses are often idealistic. In contrast to Illich, Paulo Freire sees the school as a social and historical institution inside which class conflicts take place.

In his book *La cuestión escolar: críticas y alternativas*, Jesús Palacios brings Paulo Freire, Ivan Illich, and Everett Reimer (author of *School is Dead*) together, calling them representatives of the new pedagogy of Latin America, the countries of the Third World, and of colonized societies. He distinguishes Freire from Illich and identifies Illich's position with that of Reimer. He sees in these authors an attempt to overcome the conflict between the traditional school and the new school, which he calls an "integrative triumph." According to Palacios, this vision is equally found in the work of the Soviet educator Krupskaia. With almost the same words as Paulo Freire, he denounced, at the beginning of this century, the neutral, bureaucratic school, which defended a necrophiliac education. He defended the need for a biophilic education, that is, an education that trains for life, and not for death or disease. Palacios states that the majority of teachers who ask for sick leave for psychological reasons are teachers who use authoritarian methods. Accepting the educational philosophy of Paulo Freire, he concludes, "The only way for the school to overcome its crisis is by moving from critique to transformative praxis. The task of transforming the school will be like that of Sisyphus if it is not accompanied by the transformation of society."[6]

This was also the direction indicated by Karl Marx in his *Third Thesis on Feuerbach*, when he said that the educator needed to be educated, educating his own determinations, getting to know them so that he could act on them. This was the relationship that Marx saw between the educator and society. All the work of Paulo Freire is a wide-ranging theoretical and practical demonstration of this Marxist thesis.

John Dewey and the New School

Ever since he wrote his thesis to become Professor of History and the Philosophy of Education at the University of Recife, Paulo Freire has referred to John Dewey, quoting his work *Democracy and Education*, published in Brazil in 1936. It was Anísio Teixeira[7] who introduced Dewey's work into Brazil. Paulo Freire was a great admirer of the pedagogy of Anísio Teixeira, of whose work he considered himself a disciple and with whom he agreed in his criticism of excessive centralism, connected to authoritarianism and elitism, in the Brazilian educational system.

Like John Dewey and Anísio Teixeira, Paulo Freire insists on the knowledge of the life of the local community. "What is called today surveying the local environment should also be made by the pupils, with the help of their teachers. I can't see how mathematics can fail to be taught by examining the environment. I can't see how biology and natural sciences can fail to be taught by observing the environment."

But we can find a difference in their notions of culture. For Dewey, culture is simplified as it doesn't involve the social, racial, and ethnic elements while for Paulo Freire it has an anthropological connotation as the educational action always takes place in the culture of the pupil.

What the pedagogy of Paulo Freire takes from the thinking of John Dewey is the idea of learning by doing, cooperative work, the relationship between theory and practice, the method of beginning work by talking (in the language) of the pupils. But for Paulo Freire, the goals of education are different: with his liberating vision, education should be linked to a structural change in the oppressive society, although this goal will not be reached immediately and, much less so, alone.

Vygotsky and the Revolutionary Soviet Educators

In addition to the confrontation between the thinking of Paulo Freire and Ivan Illich, Carl Rogers, and John Dewey, recent studies, like those of Vera John-Steiner,[8] show the similarity between the points of view of Paulo Freire and Lev Vygotsky in what they say about the importance of interactional approaches to alphabetization. Paulo Freire has only recently discovered the work of this great Soviet educator and linguist, whose main work, *Language and Thought*, was published in 1931.

Soon after the Russian Revolution in 1917, Vygotsky visited rural areas and collective farms, looking at differences between the communities which had been alphabetized and those which had had no educational training. He was surprised by the difference in the behavior of those who were still untouched by the transformations which were taking place and those who, as a result of their experiences on collective farms and in literacy courses, were already being changed into "subjects" in the sense of Paulo Freire. Those who had had no recent educational and social experiences tried to avoid dialogue and participation in discussion as critical persons. When asked to question visitors about life outside the village, they replied: "I can't think of anything to ask . . . in order to ask you must have knowledge and all we know is how to weed the fields."

The peasants who had taken part in the transforming process of the revolution, however, had many questions: "How can we have a better life? Why is the life of the urban worker better than that of the rural worker?" This type of change has been seen in a number of situations in which the people have begun to transform their sociolinguistic reality: Chile, Brazil, Guinea-Bissau, Cuba, Mississippi, and so on. When the people are convinced that they can change their own social reality and that they are no longer isolated or powerless, they begin to take part in dialogues, first orally and then in writing. Oral discourse is a key factor in the success or failure of the adult literacy process.

Vygotsky's theory of written language contains a description of the internal processes that characterize the production of written words. He says that the mental source of written resources is the "internal discourse" that evolves from the egocentric discourse of the child.

Vygotsky recognizes that in all human discourses the individual changes and develops his internal discourse with age and experience. Language is as enormously important in the way children become more cognitively sophisticated as it is in their increase in social affection. This is because language is the means through which children and adults systematize their perceptions.

Human beings formulate generalizations, abstractions, and other forms of thinking through words. Therefore, the words contained in the sentence "the fragile bridge over which our thoughts should travel" are historically and socially determined and, as a consequence, are formed, limited, or expanded through individual and collective experience.

Although Freire and Vygotsky have lived at different times and in different hemispheres, their approaches both emphasize fundamental aspects which are relative to interconnected social and educational changes. While Vygotsky focuses on the psychological dynamic, Freire concentrates on educational strategies and the analysis of language. As for the transformation of internal discourse into written discourse, the proposals of both could be powerful tools not just in basic literacy schemes but also in programs to teach more advanced written skills.

At different times and in different places, both saw the need to associate the conquest of the word with the conquest of history.

The idea of learning through practice is also found in Anton Semionovitch Makarenko,[9] whose educational experience was developed in the twenties and thirties when he was the director of "corrective" educational institutions, the first of them being Gorky Colony, which was designed for children and abandoned young people. Humility, simplicity, and optimism are qualities common to both educators.

There is also a relationship between the theories of Paulo Freire and those of Pistrak,[10] especially Freire's idea of the self-organization of children at school and the idea of involvement and of the social and political analysis of reality as part of the school curriculum. Pistrak's idea that pupils should take part in the "general assembly" is very near to the idea developed later by Freire in relation to the participation of the students in the cultural circles.

The Complexity and the Universal Dimension of the Work of Paulo Freire

Paulo Freire has been influenced in different ways: his humanistic thinking was inspired by the personalism of Emmanuel Mounier[11] and by the existentialism, phenomenology and Marxism. However, it can't be said that Paulo Freire is just eclectic. He integrates the fundamental elements of these philosophical doctrines without repeating them in a mechanical or biased way.

The association between humanism and Marxism, between Christian and Marxist themes, enriches his texts and enables them to be read by a wide public. His thinking represents the synthesis of different sources. This fact gives a problem to the beginning reader who is making a general reading.

Rosiska Darcy de Oliveira and Pierre Dominicé have said that there is the risk that each reader might take from Paulo Freire what will serve his own interests. Thus the Latin American reader of Paulo Freire

will understand Paulo Freire in terms of his political struggle or his practice of social movement inside this socioeconomic setting. If he is Catholic, he will identify with the humanistic orientation and he will feel on home ground through the influence of the philosophers who influenced Paulo Freire's thinking. If the reader is Marxist, he will recognize a problem which the contemporary currents of Marxist thinking (Gramsci, Lukács, Marcuse) have accustomed him to. If the reader is an educationalist, he will find the emphasis on the liberation which characterizes progressive trends in educational thinking today. Only those who have a little of all these characteristics at the same time or who have passed through these different "stages" or who have suffered these different influences can really understand Freire's intention and the totality of his intellectual development (cheminement).[12]

Paulo Freire's pedagogy has acquired a universal meaning since the oppressed/oppressor relationship which he examined occurs throughout the world and his theories have been enriched with the most varied experiences from many countries.

As Antonio Faundez says in his book on the process of alphabetization and postalphabetization in São Tomé and Príncipe, a large part of the theoretical contribution of Paulo Freire came as a result of his experiences in the Northeast of Brazil and in other Latin American countries. However, the work he performed in various African countries also helped to enrich his practice and pedagogical theories, making him rethink certain initial methods and ideas, which, from a political and pedagogical point of view, were open to criticism.

Juan Eduardo Garcia-Huidobro, in his thesis which was presented in 1976, in Belgium, analyzes the theory of conscientization as the most representative alternative for Latin American liberation, parting from the educational thinking of Antonio Gramsci. Others have compared Paulo Freire to Fanon, Memmi, and Amílcar Cabral.

Similarly, his theories have given rise to the most varied forms of practice. This is the case, for example, of the bilingual application of his method by Isabel Hernández with the Mapuche Indians in the south of Chile. Six percent of the Chilean population are, at the moment, Mapuches, that is to say, six hundred thousand people, of whom one hundred thousand live in the large urban centers and the rest in rural areas.

Isabel Hernádez worked with members of Paulo Freire's team in Chile. Her original methodology is based on the latent bilingualism that America offers, uniting the language of the conqueror with the language of the marginalized, impoverished, and rebellious Indian. Her

FIGURE 12

An original homage. On a visit that Moacir Gadotti made to Stockholm (Sweden) with Paulo Freire, he discovered a marble sculpture of himself in a public square. Paulo Freire was with 6 other contemporary figures who have performed exceptional work in the struggle for peace and solidarity. The work was made by the Swedish Sculptor Pye Engström, who presents it in the following way: "This sculpture is a sofa. Please, sit down for a while! The people I chose to the part of this work have great meaning for me and represent important principles of our time. This sofa is a document of 1972, a fine a time when I decided that important people would make up the sofa.

From right to left they are:

PABLO NERUDA - the Chilean, so we don't forget the Chilean people and their struggle against Facism.

GEORG BORGSTRÖM - for his work in showing us that the earth is fragile and that its resources are not inexhaustible.

ANGELA DAVIS - for her struggle against racism.

MAO TSETUNG - for having led the struggle of the Chinese people against hunger and humiliation.

SARA LIDMAN - for the support she gave to the people of Vietnam in their struggle against imperialism, through her Literary creation.

PAULO FREIRE - for having formulated a pedagogy in the service of the oppressed, which will help people to create a new society.

ELISE OTTESEN-JENSEN - for her work in the defense of the right of women to decide their lives and the right of children to be born wanted.

These seven people defend the tormented and the oppressed of the world".

alphabetizing method uses conscientizing resources that try to take the Indian out of the limited world to which he has been condemned for centuries by the European invader, freeing him from his unfortunate inheritance.

In addition to the countries in which Paulo Freire has directly applied his own ideas, many others have borrowed his methods and achieved positive results.

Mexico is an example. To reduce its number of illiterates to 12 percent, it has used various educational programs, among them Paulo Freire's method.

In 1987 Paulo Freire was at the Faulty of Humanities and Educational Sciences of Cochabamba, Bolivia, with his popular education team from Campinas, Brazil (Débora Mazza, Adriano Nogueira, José Lima, and Luís Longuini). This visit enabled a study and exchange of experiences on popular education, the role of the universities in the Third World, and the place of theories on popular education in the contemporary pedagogical thinking of Latin America.

In Brazil, the alphabetization programs financed by the federal government, like MOBRAL (Movimento Brasileiro de Alfabetização Brazilain Movement for Literacy), have ignored Paulo Freire's method, in spite of their using some of his techniques. The method has only been applied in grassroots ecclesiastical communities and in rural areas. The "New" Republic did not take any notice of his proposals although he has never refused any invitation from the large number of town councils and other public institutions in Brazil who have asked him for his help.

Critique, Self-Critique, and Dialectic Conception

The challenging ideas of Paulo Freire and their worldwide repercussion cannot please everyone. In spite of his enormous capacity for dialogue and his humility, he has been violently criticized, especially by members of the bourgeoisie.

We can reproduce the complete text one of these attacks. It is the leader of the *Jornal do Brasil*, June 26, 1985, entitled "Ideological ABC." Paulo Freire didn't make a reply, despite the enormous insistence of his old friend, Lauro de Oliveira Lima.

Mr. Paulo Freire would be of great help to the new generations if he could show himself in flesh and bone more often to explain his ideas out loud—or rather, his fixed idea. Then young people would be better able to see the distance between the man and the myth.

The author (or codifier) of a method of adult literacy which has only been used in the most backward countries of the Third World, Mr. Paulo Freire was democratically invited to a discussion with technicians from MOBRAL, which is looking for a goal which is more in keeping with the educational needs of Brazil in the eighties.

Suggestions were hoped for. Instead, the guest repeated old, rancid clichés, which even some socialist countries have stopped using. Demonstrating that he lives more in the past than for tomorrow, and that in his spirit there is more room for resentment than for generosity, the guest began by accusing MOBRAL of taking over his method in order to distort it and transform it into an instrument of a capitalistic alphabetization.

It is this distinction made by Freire of a bourgeois alphabetization versus a proletarian alphabetization that makes the car of common sense swerve and skid. For mortal human beings, alphabetization is no more than learning the skills of reading and writing to a point at which they become functional. This is a conception which, as it is so simple, doesn't enter the simplism of a world vision which reduces all realities to the Manicheism of the class struggle.

Thousands of years before capitalism, socialism, and the appearance of Mr. Paulo Freire, societies with the most diverse structures were already teaching their children and adults how to read and write— and they didn't need any ideological element to be successful. What has our famous educator to say about this?

This leader seems to be more a recognition of Paulo Freire's work in favor of the oppressed, especially in the Third World, something Paulo Freire has never denied.

We have already seen that the thinking of Paulo Freire does not apply only to the countries of the Third World, nor can it be reduced just to a method of alphabetization. The leader writer is unaware that, long before Marx, bourgeois economists like Adam Smith recognized the existence of the class struggle. It would be a gross error to ignore this fact. The leader writer seems to belong to a school of educational thinking called functionalism, which reduces education to the transmission and assimilation of formal content.

The critiques that the bourgeoisie makes nowadays are the same as in 1962. An example is Sandra Cavalcanti, a member of the Constituent Assembly, who, at that time, made up a dossier on Paulo Freire at the request of Carlos Lacerda, governor of the state of Rio de Janeiro. This dossier said that his method had, at its beginning, the support of "communists with a police record." She describes her impression on seeing Madalena, Paulo's daughter, then sixteen, going to give classes *barefoot* (emphasis hers) so she could identify with the pupils, and her impression on seeing Madalena'a boyfriend, who was also a "teacher."

Cavalcanti relates the class on the word *lombriga* (roundworm): "A poster with the word, a poster with hungry people. A dialogue heard in the class: 'What is the cause of the roundworm?' Reply: 'Latifúndio'. . .and not a single word about hygiene." In this way, she simplifies and decontextualizes a class, in addition to extracting certain aspects which confirm her class vision.

Some criticisms have been the result of a lack of information or because of bad faith, but the majority have been through ideological and political disagreement. Some, however, use the critiques of the work of Paulo Freire to try to advance further, looking for extrapolations, a better understanding, to learn and continue.

His philosopy has been criticized by the Cardenal of Porto Alegre (South Brazil), Dom Vicente Scherer, because it "fails to conciliate or harmonize with the principles of the Christian doctrine, irreconcilably clashing and contradicting with them," and "accepts Hegelian dialectics and the Marxist interpretation of history."

His educational philosophy has also been criticized from an opposite direction by Vanilda Pereira Paiva, in *Paulo Freire e o nacionalismo desenvolvimentista*, which placed him in the line of thinking of ISEB (Higher Institute for Brazilian Studies), which, according to Paiva, was a right-wing ideology inasmuch as it proposed a development based on an alliance between classes.

Paulo Freire disagrees with this interpretation as he doesn't see just an "ideology factory" at ISEB. ISEB was marked by its time, giving priority to the anti-imperialist and antifeudal struggle. This struggle was a proposal of the Brazilian Communist party, which defended a pact between classes. Although she doesn't take into account all of Paulo Freire's work, Vanilda Pereira Paiva makes a detailed study of the time when the ideas from ISEB were popular. As a man of his time, Paulo Freire influenced and was influenced by this period. But he continued living.

Sílvia Maria Manfredi, in *Política e educação popular*, states that Paulo Freire, in spite of denying the oppressive society and the corresponding forms of domination, doesn't explicate the type of society he would like to construct. Moreover, he doesn't clarify the nature of the revolution which he would like to unleash and the socioeconomic bases that should support the new power structure. She therefore concludes that Paulo Freire is "idealistic" and "liberal," not refusing the capitalist system, and distancing himself from the theeoretical and methodological orientations which are based on the presuppositions of historical and dialectic materialism.

Paulo Freire has been charged by many Marxist readers for not referring explicitly to the class struggle but rather speaking in more general terms of the struggle between the oppressed and the oppressors. On his return to Brazil, the newspaper *Movimento* (Movement) referred to these criticisms and asked him (13 August 1979):

> Some recently published theses have publicly argued that you have said that education must serve for the oppressed person to become conscientized that he is oppressed and that he should struggle against the oppressor, but that you use categories like oppressed and oppressor, dominated and dominator, without ever entering into class relationships. What do you think of this?

The reply of Paulo Freire:

In 1973 I gave an interview which I published in *Ação cultural e outros escritos* (Cultural action and other writings), in which I replied to this question, which was also answered in books written afterwards. I remember that the first time that it was said that I didn't talk about classes I reread *Pedagogy of the Oppressed* noting the number of times I talked about social class. There were thirty-five references, if I'm not mistaken, which doesn't necessarily mean that I've been clear. I'm under the impression that I've made myself clearer in other works. On the other hand, there are doctoral students who write their Ph.D. thesis without reading all my books, and there are students with so much energy that they don't even write. . . . On frequent occasions these students base themselves on just one of Paulo Freire's books without making a global analysis.

Paulo Freire is not just the most widely read educator in Brazil today. He has another record: the educator with the most labels. He has been called "national-developmentalist," "new schoolist," "inductivist," "spontaneist," "nondirectivist," "Catholic neoanarchist," and so on.

Paulo Freire doesn't reply to these critiques directly. He limits himself to explaining his positions better without entering into the sterile and destructive arguments which, the majority of times, just try to deliberately destroy his proposals in their attempt to make his thinking inviable as an institutional practice.

In *Comunicação e cultura*, Venício Artur de Lima discusses the "paradoxes" contained in the concept of communication and the impossibility of antagonists holding a dialogue, which, according to him, makes the possibility of the oppressed freeing themselves from their oppressors unfeasible. Paulo Freire clarifies his position on this problem in *Pedagogia: diálogo e conflito.*

Some critics have tried to show that Paulo Freire's first writings are "idealistic" and that his conception of "dialogue," founded on Christian humanism, is subjective and reformist.

As a man of his time, Paulo Freire admits that he has occasionally been ingenuous. To those who consider that he was indecisive in his view of class relations, he says that there are no finished models of society as the social structure is always in motion. Oppression does not take place only on the social plane but also on the individual level. And it is just on this level that authoritarianism can be seen. And it is just here that oppression must begin to be fought, that is, where it is nearest to us.

Paulo Freire replies to those left-wing intellectuals who criticize him for having defended the New School by saying that the New School made important and effective methodological contributions. However, the New School did no more than this. Freire has criticized the capitalist means of production that the New School didn't criticize. To do this, content would have to be changed. But more important is the openness that the specialists, the organizers of the content of education, must have, which is a result of the direct contact with reality and respect for the creative capacity of the pupils.

That task of reproducing the dominant ideology, which the dominant classes demand from systematic education, doesn't exhaust the role of the school. Within the school there are other tasks which can be performed, and one of them is just this: to contradict this task, to demythologize ideological reproduction.

In the cases of Nicaragua and Cuba, the central question is to confront, through education, aspects of the previous ideology which are found inside the same educational practice. There is a dialectic game of contradictions between the myths of the dominant ideology and the revolutionary dreams. At times, these myths and dreams are found in the same person. The problem is that ideology cannot be changed through martial laws. If it were so, everything would be easy.

Fidel Castro, at the first major congress of educators in Cuba, in January 1986, took a dialectic position when he said that the congress could take place because the revolution had taken place. The radical transformation of society of the structures of society had made a new understanding of pedagogy possible.

One cannot hope that, when the mode of production is changed, all social relationships will mechanically change. Therefore, it is necessary to avoid the reproduction of the authoritarian character typical of capitalist production.

When asked about the traditional elements which educational methods still maintain in Cuba and in Nicaragua, Fidel Castro replied by saying that a revolution can't be understood mechanically but historically. History cannot be transformed by changing people's ideas, however clarified they may be. It is transformed dialectically, that is, in a contradictory way. Because of this, it takes a lot of energy and time to undo the old and make the new. If this relationship were mechanical, on the day after the revolutionary triumph, the new man and woman and the new education would be ready. But this relationship is historical rather than mechanical.

The preservation of traditional methods of education in a revolutionary context signifies the distance between dream and practice. One of the revolutionary struggles is the struggle for the renovation of methods and procedures at the same time as the content of education is renewed.

Paulo Freire incorporated Marxist ideas in his thinking, above all from his experience in exile. In his book *Pedagogia: diálogo e conflito*, he makes this point explicit.

Dialogue and conflict are shown as strategies of the oppressed. Dialogue takes place between equals and those with differences, never between those who are antagonistic. Between antagonists, there is a conflict, or, when it is greater, a pact. There can also be a conflict between equals, but this is of another type: there is fundamental respect which, in one way or another, keeps them together. One can live with different people but not with those who are antagonistic.

There is no doubt that Paulo Freire has made a decisive contribution to the dialectic conception of education. The official authoritarian pedagogy and liberal theoreticians (both conservatives and progressives) challenge his ideas exactly for this emancipating and dialectic characteristic. Whether we accept his educational ideas or not, his thinking has been a milestone in Brazilian and international pedagogy.

The contribution of Paulo Freire cannot be reduced merely to the popular adult literacy schemes. His contribution overtakes his method and is situated in a much wider view of education and the theory of knowledge.

I have often been asked what Paulo Freire's method consists of and where exactly one can find the faithfulness to a position which has guided and still guides his work. My reply has usually been the same: being faithful to the educational proposal of Paulo Freire doesn't consist of repeating it mechanically or reproducing it uncritically. Paulo Freire holds the mechanism, the pose of submissive and obedient disciples, in horror. Being faithful to Paulo Freire means, before anything else, reinventing him and reinventing oneself like him. Besides, it is in this that the element of triumph in the dialectic consists: it is neither the copy or the negation of the past, of the path others have followed. It is in his transformation, through which there is something fundamental and original in him, into a new qualitative synthesis.

Conclusion

Both in public and in private, in the classroom or preparing an article, Paulo Freire is always the same, generally happy and in a good mood. His jokes reveal a playful spirit and also elements of his personality. For example, he sometimes calls my house, and, when my wife answers the telephone, he says: "Is this Ra, Re, Ri, Ro, Ru?" My wife, Rejane (Re), was surprised the first time; then we found out that he also does this with other people. Cristina, his granddaughter, recieved a telephone call asking her if it was the house of "Cras, Cres, Cris, Cros, Crus." No doubt, her grandfather, with his mania of the alphabetizer, was trying to multiply phonemes.

If one day the reader rings the doorbell of his house and is not answered, it is quite probable that what is happening is what has happened to me on several occasions: he'll be listening to his favorite tangos played at full volume.

On one occasion I asked the great student of the work of Paulo Freire, Carlos Alberto Torres, from Buenos Aires, what this love of Paulo Freire for the tango, such tragic music, meant.

Carlos Alberto, a spare-time singer of tangos, told me that the tango is not just this; it is also, and fundamentally, an urban song and social criticism.

As urban song, the tango expresses the weakness and the richness of human interaction, where passion, deception, and the need for affection are all mixed.

As social criticism, the tango contests, as it takes on an anarchist perspective in the face of authority, the

FIGURE 13

Paulo Freire today.

decadence of a civilization or a society controlled by a conservative oligarchy. It expresses the strong social pressure of the lumpenproletariat, of the first generation of the children of immigrants who are looking for access to all the social goods, to wealth, to a new social space.

Therefore, when we understand the tango as the bottled-up expression of machismo, of suffering in the face of deception, of the need to reflect the dignity of someone who has suffered misery, in short, as the manifestation of the crisis of an urban civilization, it becomes easier to understand why Paulo Freire likes tangos.

Torres, at the end of his explanation, wondered if he was not overintellectualizing this idea. Paulo Freire himself has never worried about explaining his liking of tangos. He just listens to them.

I would like to finish this book by talking a little more about Paulo Freire's personality.

At the moment I am writing, he is fully occupied—writing, learning, participating—and so this work will always be incomplete. Rather than an original work on Paulo Freire, this book is a first reading, an invitation to understand him better, to walk at his side.

Despite my great admiration for Paulo Freire, I wouldn't like this book to be considered an apology for him and his ideas. My commitment is with transparency and with truth.

The great book from which we all learn is reality, the world. And the world and reality are contradictory.

Paulo Freire also suffers frustrations, like all of us. He can leave a seminar angrily if he thinks that he hasn't reached his objectives. He goes through moments of anguish because the world is not the way he dreamed it should be. He also often finds it difficult to believe that other people cannot accept him. He becomes angry although he is an even-tempered man. He's proud, despite being democratic. He's passionate, but he doesn't separate his passion from his ideas. He likes to say that he is a man of his time, but like every historical and participating man of the present, he's afraid of being overtaken by time.

Paulo Freire is alive and working, changing with history and making plans.

He spent some days in Recife thinking about the possibility of permanently going back there. He ended up deciding to restart life in São Paulo, without leaving Recife, with new plans for his life and for the development of his work.

But he imposed one condition on himself: that he would only do what would combine both work and pleasure at the same time. Doing what he liked. Setting up the school of tenderness, of happiness. He wants to prove to his colleagues and pupils that studying—like living—is pleasant, though often tough.

I have often been asked why Paulo Freire didn't take up his position again at the Federal University of Pernambuco, where he was Senior Professor until 1964?

With the 1979 amnesty, the Brazilian government demanded that every exile, in order to return to his job in Brazil, had to undergo a kind of "test of dangerousness," given by a commission nominated by the dictatorship. Paulo refused to undergo this test and was thus adversely affected financially for many years.

With the coming of the so-called New Republic in 1985, an amendment to the Amnesty Law automatically gave him his job back. In 1987 Paulo complained that his job had not been given him back, and it was done that very year. Immediately after, he asked for his retirement, which he had a right to, "not to take up the places of the young people," as he said on requesting it.

In the year that followed Elza's death, which took place in October 1986, he hardly wrote anything, apart from letters addressed to her, which he didn't want to publish. One of the few jobs that he accepted was that of being a consultant to UNICEF. At the end of 1987, he asked to return to work at the Catholic University of São Paulo, thus returning to teaching and research.

In 1985, the Federal University of Pernambuco (old University of Recife), called for the nominal reintegration of Paulo Freire into the university staff which he left in 1964 into exile. He was nominally reintegrated the following year, and immediately retired. According to a declaration by Paulo Freire during that period he retired "in order to leave room for the younger generation." In 1981 he also retired, due to his age of seventy, from the University of Campinas where he had initiated his work in 1980. Since then he has continued to administer seminaries in the Catholic University of São Paulo, discussing above all, student programs, their thesis work, and their practice. He remains very active, teaching courses, giving conferences, and working as advisor to popular education groups and universities.

Among his present projects, there are four that I would like to emphasize, which are connected with the act of writing: (1) *Letters to Cristina*, a book of reflections (but not only this), which is already being worked on, in which education continues to be the central theme; (2) an essay on Amílcar Cabral, a "pedagogy of revolution," in which he makes references to Fidel Castro and Che Guevara; (3) a rereading of *Pedagogy of the Oppressed*, twenty years after, reflecting on the journey of this book around the world. There are many reflections and interesting stories about *Pedagogy of the Oppressed*, which has gained its own independence. Paulo Freire doesn't intend to rewrite it but relearn it at a certain distance. This work is finished and will be published shortly with the title *The Pedagogy of Hope: Reviving the Pedagogy of the Oppressed*; (4) an anthology of his main texts, some of them rewritten and others rearranged and joined together. This book would be used in the initial training of the young educator.

Paulo Freire has never written for children but would like to. Who knows, maybe one day he will.

In a speech in Paris, on December 12th, 1991, I heard Paulo Freire affirm in front of an immense audience: "I experience a fantastic radical ambiguity."[1] Afterwards, he continued to say that he was a man markedly influenced by contemporary European thought, but in the Latin American historical context. Paulo Freire does not understand European thought like a European, but like a Brazilian—to be more precise, as a Northeasterner.

I believe that Paulo Freire was able to, on the one hand, demystify the dreams of pedagogism of the sixties, which pretended that the school, at least in Latin America, could achieve everything, and, on other hand, was able to overcome the pessimism of the seventies, when it was said that the school was merely an ideological apparatus of the state. Overcoming ingenuous pedagogism and negativist pessimism, Freire remained faithful to a utopia of dreaming possible dreams.

In concluding this book I wonder, what future the thought of Paulo Freire has. I believe that the future of Paulo Freire's work is closely linked to the future of popular education as a general conception of education.

Little more than twenty years after the *Pedagogy of the Oppressed*, popular education, marked by this seminal work, continues to consitute the greatest contribution that Latin American thought has made to universal pedagogical thought. Popular education is a theoretical framework which continues to inspire numerous experiences, not only in Latin America, but all over the world, not only in Third World countries, but in advanced industrial countries, and in very distinct realities.

Paulo Freire was influenced by the very movement in which he is inserted, and to which he has made and continues to make an enormous contribution.

Popular education has passed through various stages. It is a dynamic movement, inspired by various visions, which form an immense mosaic. Not all these visions identify with the thought of Paulo Freire, but many refer to him, from the guerrilla optimism of the Nicaraguan literacy campaign, through nonformal community schools, to public school experiences in education.

All of these examples demonstrate the universal extension of Paulo Freire's thought, which has no parallels in the history of pedagogical ideas.

The work of Paulo Freire should continue spreading in multiple directions, perhaps even in antagonistic ways. He will not have any control over this phenomenon, just as Marx cannot be held responsible for Marxism, or for all that has been done in his name. And the positive and negative criticisms should continue as well.

I usualy divide these critics into two distinct groups: (1) those who refuse to accept Freire's ideas due to prejudice or due to ideological and methodological motives; (2) those who criticize his thought but at the same time accept his presuppositions.

The first prefer to call Freire an "idealist," "popular progressivist," "nondirectivist," "Catholic neoanarchist," and even "authoritarian." The labels are many. Paulo Freire's thought has provoked a great deal of argument, especially with those who do not accept his proposals.

Among those who accept his pressuppositions, some can be called "orthodox Freirians": that is, those who understand Freire's thought as complete in itself, and which does not require the contribution of any other school of thought. These are in the minority and we can consider them ingenuous. They are the ones who make his work into myth. Those who are accustomed to working more closely to Freire and his work can be called "heterodox Freirians" as Freire himself is.[2] This is because they add to the thought of Paulo Freire other important contributions in universal pedagogy. And since such contributions are numerous, at times irreconcilable, many currents of thought have been formed based upon Freire's work. All of them rely on the legacy of Paulo Freire, but interpret him in different ways.

I consider myself a student of Paulo Freire, in the same way I consider myself a student of the work of Marx, without being a Marxist. I attempt to approximate the thought of Paulo Freire to other contributions. It was in this manner that during the seventies, I sought to understand Paulo Freire as a foundation for a Marxist pedagogy of freedom, joining the category of conflict to his pedagogy of dialogue. This can be seen in my preface to Freire's book, *Educação e mudança* published in Brazil in 1979. Later I debated the theme of the relationship between a pedagogy of dialogue and one of conflict in the book I published in 1985, *Pedagogia: diálogo e conflito*. I agree, along with Marilena Chaui, that "it is a privilege of democracy to be the only political regime that considers conflict legitimate and relies upon it for the realization of politics."[3]

In my experience of working alongside Freire for the past two decade—in particular as his Cabinet Chief in the administration of the Municipal Secretariat of Education in São Paulo and especially coordinating the Literacy Movement in São Paulo (MOVA-SP)—I sought to demonstrate to Freire that, given the historical conditions of centralization and authoritarianism of Brazilian institutions, it is necessary to seek the autonomy of the school at all levels. A point of divergence that I hold with Freire is on this particular issue of school autonomy: he advocates a more directive role on the part of educational administrators, while I maintain that even the proposal of autonomy must be generated from within the school itself, thus reducing the influence upon the school. In my opinion, the pedagogical proposals of the Secretariat should be the proposals which come from schools.[4]

As he told me in a private conversation (August 28, 1992), despite this difference in opinions, our friendship continues. Difference in theoretical and practical points of view, in order to be productive, must respect what is fundamental: the individual person. Divergencies do not imply disrespect between persons. On the contrary, to diverge and maintain respect manifests a high level of civilization to which everyone should aspire.[5]

Some years ago, someone maliciously stated that Paulo Freire had ceased to think. Quite the opposite! To the desperation of his detractors, Paulo Freire continues thinking, acting, producing, publishing,[6] reading, working, participating, and fighting. He continues in love with the world. Paulo Freire continues to get involved in new projects. He remains indignant with the lack of freedom, and with political corruption. In short, Paulo Freire is as alive as his own thought.

Epilogue:
Education at the
End of This Century

Dialogue with Paulo Freire

We end with an interview between the author and
Paulo Freire about this book and the prospects for
education at the end of this century.

Moacir Gadotti: I wrote this book with the intention of
recovering the memory of an educator
of this century. I tried to relate his work
to that of other contemporary educators. But this is not merely an interest
in the past; it is also an attempt to
construct a pedagogy for the future,
and I think that this is your pedagogy.
The orientation that we follow is to
continually ask ourselves what we can
do, today, within the human and
historical circumstances in which we
place education, to leave the world a
little bit better than we found it.
    We would like to invite teachers
who are becoming qualified to collectively take part in this world of
solidarity, a world which may receive
many names, but which we can now

see, without being more specific, as a world which is fuller of happiness, love, and will to live.

How do you see the contribution of the educator today in the construction of this society? In what ways should he be trained?

Paulo Freire: I would like to begin not by talking just to you but by talking through you, to the readers of this excellent book you are just finishing. I would like to have a talk with these young people who are just finishing their training and who are part of a process of training that should be permanent. I would begin by telling them of the pleasure I have in having this talk with them through you, and then I would say that your question has a lot to do with what I always call "this end of century," using this expression to mean something that we are already living right now and going to carry on living intensely, so that we can create and build things we don't yet have. . . .

I think that one of the good things that a young man or woman, an adult, an old man, any one of us, has as a historical task is to assume his time, to integrate and insert himself in his own epoch. I would like to once again appeal to the young people who are going to talk with me through you to tell them that the best way for someone to assume his own time is to lucidly understand history as a possibility.

What does this mean? At one moment of your text, you refer, without necessarily quoting, to a fundamental affirmation of Marx in which he said that man—and I would add women—makes history. Yes, of course, but man makes history from a reality which he finds, and only from this.

When I tell a young person, "In order for you to assume your time and to become a man or woman of your time, you must first understand history as a possibility," what I mean is that what Marx said is absolutely correct. I apologize to the young people for saying that Marx was correct, but, as I am not a slave of Marx's thinking, I believe that from time to time I should say that he was right or that it seems he was wrong.

It is absolutely certain that men and women make history from given concrete circumstances, from an already existing structure inside which we find ourselves. But this time and this space must be a time and space of *possibility*, and not a time and space that mechanically determine us.

What I mean to say by this is that, while I understand history as a possibility, I also understand its impossibility.

I then discover that the future that we talk about is that which you are referring to. The future is not pregiven.

When a generation arrives in the world, its future is not predetermined or preestablished. On the other hand, neither is the future a pure repetition of an unsatisfactory present. The future is something which comes on, and this "coming on" means that the future exists to the extent that I or we change the present. And it is through changing the present that we make the future. Therefore, I'm sure that history is a possibility and not a determination.

Now, if history is this possibility, if I assume myself in my own time, I must discover what the fundamental tasks of this time are. And this is what you are asking me now: what to say to these young people?

I clearly couldn't pretend to tell them what their tasks should be, but I can tell them what I have assumed as a task, and what has been the task of my generation. . . I think that the most fundamental task that we have, at this end of century, and whose understanding has come a long time before the end of the century, is the task of liberation. But it is not even a task of liberation.

I think that freedom is a natural quality of the human being. I would even say, more radically, that freedom makes part of the nature of life, whether it is animal or vegetable. The tree that grows and bends to look for the sun makes a movement of freedom, but one that is conditioned to its species, merely a vital impulse, not the instinct of freedom of a dog.

We should ask ourselves today about the task of liberation in terms of the restoration of freedom, or in terms of the invention of a freedom which is not yet allowed. Then I would say that this is becoming a permanent, historical task. I wouldn't say that it is the biggest task, or the only one, but it is the central one which the others will join. I think that it is fundamental that, understanding history as a possibility, the educator should discover education as a possibility to the extent that education is deeply historical.

When we understand education as a possibility, we discover that education has limits. And it is exactly because it is limitable, or ideologically, economically, socially, and culturally limited that it is effective. So I would say to the educators who today are eighteen, and who are going to enter the next century at the beginning of their creative lives, that, even recognizing that education in the next century is not going to be the key for the transformation of the concrete for re-creation and for the retaking of freedom, even though they know that this will not be the case, they should be convinced of the efficacy of the educational practice as a fundamental element in the process of recovering freedom.

Moacir Gadotti: Paulo, doesn't the generation that is coming, this generation that is eighteen, nineteen, twenty, today, and that will build the future society, when they refer the future as a possibility, speak less of sociological categories and more of ethical and anthropological categories. These are related to love, friendship, transparency, political will.

The education that is starting with these young people talks a lot abou t life,dividuality, the body. The body is rediscovered in a progressive way. It seems that the struggle for liberation in some past generations failed to value the bodies of people; the struggle was more social. And suddenly there's something new happening, which has been brought by this generation that wants freedom with pleasure, love, and the body. How do you see this, this molecular revolution, in the expression of Felix Guattari, the French philosopher, that young people want to make with their bodies?

Paulo Freire:

I think that your pedagogy has given a lot of value to the different, the person, the individual, in this struggle. I think that, because of this, your ideas are today even more pertinent than in the past, because of this recovery of the different. You value the contribution of each individual in the process of the transformation of history. I would like you to comment on this a little.

I would even apologize to the readers as what I'm going to say might not seem not very humble, but it's very connected to what you've said. You said, in your role as an analyst, that you feel that at least some of these ideas, or the spirit of the pedagogy itself, might even be received better today.

It's true. I was recently in the United States, and I again saw that it is not by chance that *Pedagogy of the Oppressed* is in its twenty-seventh edition, and in Spanish, in its thirty-fifth. This has got something to do with what you said.

You make a clear statement, you accept, you embrace a certain type of comprehension of the world, a comprehension of the struggle. It is clear that you don't just sympathize with this understanding of the body, but that you understand it, and that you understand the role of the body.

I recently saw in a qualification exam how you thrill when you deal with the work of a candidate who talks about the problem of the body, but emphasizing, however—and you did this very well—that after all, "*the body is what I do.*" That is to say, what I do makes my body.

What I think great in all this is, as what I do makes my body what it is, my body is being because because I do something that belongs to it. The importance of the body can therefore not be discussed: the present-day body memorizes its struggle for freedom. The body, after all, desires, points, announces, protests, bends, stands up, draws, and remakes the world.

None of us, neither you nor I, are saying that the transformation is made through an individual body. No, because *the body is also socially constructed.* But it happens that it has an enormous importance. And this importance has to do with a certain *sensuality.*

I'll confess something to you: I can't believe in a revolution that denies love, that puts the question of love between brackets. In this I'm a follower of Che Guevara. Love and revolution are married together. There's a lot of sensuality that the body keeps and makes explicit, which is even connected to the cognitive capacity.

I think it absurd to distance the rigorous act of knowing the world from the passionate ability to know. I personally am not just in love with the world but also with the process itself of getting to know the world.

Moacir Gadotti: Paulo, what has been told to young people, above all by the means of communication, is that to be revolutionary is to be serious, ugly, dull, moldy. This is the idea of revolution that is broadcast, that the revolutionary. . .

Paulo Freire: . . . makes love with his nightshirt on.

Moacir Gadotti: Exactly. This pedagogy that we want to build with the young people who are going to make the new pedagogy, with the young people who, shortly, will also write their books and build a revolutionary pedagogy, which will certainly not be a rancid pedagogy. . .

Paulo Freire: It could be, but I don't think it will. You see, a man like Georges Snyders, the great French educator, who for me has one of the best conceptions of what a pedagogy should be like at this end of century. He is a socialist who has made a clear Marxist choice and who has a creative loyalty to Marxist thinking. His last book, *La joie à l'école (Happiness at School) is a hymn to joy.* What he does is to invite the education to make happiness through education. The school he describes, the school of his dreams, is an exciting school. But it's no less serious because of this. In Snyders this would be absurd. It would be absurd to imagine that he could defend the lack of seriousness.

I agree with you. The young people who are reading us today are not going to build a weak and loose pedagogy. But I think that the task of freedom, the task of liberation, history as a possibility, the understanding of the conscious and sensual body, full of life, this all demands a *pedagogy of contentment*.

This makes me remember an invitation I had to take part in some seminars in Cuba, which I enjoyed a lot. There, I met a young teacher of Marxist ethics at the University of Havana, who gave me a text she had written about love, in which love is discussed from a Marxist ethical point of view. She had given her text to the young people at the University of Havana, and she told me that these university students demanded, in the discussion they had with her, a more explicit kind of love: they wanted freedom to love and loving to make them free. The girls, for example, complained about the lack of affection in a relationship, the lack of tenderness on the part of the young men. They wanted more affection, a certain playful and loving affection.

So I think that *lovingness, affection,* first of all, don't weaken in any way whatsoever the seriousness of studying and of producing; and secondly, they don't get in the way of political and social responsibility. I've lived my life lovingly.

Moacir Gadotti: From what you've said, I can see that we're already living the *education of this end of century,* which is an education that accomplishes its essential task of the reproduction and of the construction of knowledge with a new perspective. The traditional school insists that one only learns with effort, through punishment, the stick.

Today, by contrast, young people demand beauty and attractiveness, an integration between what they study and their lives. They revolt against authoritarianism. But this is not exactly what the Greeks called *paidéia,* an "integral education," and what Marx called omnilateral education.

The construction of the education of the future takes us back to the past, to something original there was in the beginning. But today it has acquired a much more social connotation than in Greece, where it was extremely individualistic. Today it is integrated in the joyful construction of the collective.

But let me ask another question: the school that we want for our children and grandchildren, and which we want for everyone, is not just a happy school but a *popular, autonomous public school.* This is the school of our dreams. It might not totally come true, but it is already being built, inside the elitist and capitalist school.

The public school that we want to build is not just an extension of the bourgeois public school for everyone because we know that this bourgeois school is elitist and therefore can't reach everyone. Therefore we can talk about the popular public school, that is, a school for all, with a popular management and a new quality. How do you see the birth of this school today? How can you see the new emerging from the old?

Paulo Freire: I see this as one of the unusual things of our time or as one of the reasons of being for certain unusual things of our time. I would tell the young people who are reading this book that, by taking part in the adventure of this serious, rigorous and joyful school, they should never fail to think about the *serious act of studying,* that they should never confuse this happiness with the easy happiness of not doing, which is where the traditional school also went wrong. It is not necessary to make the tables any more rigid than the hardness that wood gives them; it's not necessary to harden the posture of the children; it's not necessary to put a collar and tie on the child so that he, already suffering, can learn. Certainly not. But on the other hand, things can't be loosened to such an extent that the child gets lost just in the toy, just in being happy.

Knowing is really a difficult task, but it's necessary for the child to realize that, as it is difficult, the very process of studying becomes attractive. I also think that it would be wrong to tell the student that there is an understanding of happiness in the act of studying. The important thing is that the child realizes that the act of studying is difficult, demanding, but pleasant right from the beginning.

Moacir Gadotti: Very much so, Paulo. What Georges Snyders says in his book *La joie à l'école* is that there is no separation between the *cognitive* and the *affective*. He shows that the educator at this end of century is he who manages to put into practice this dialectic unity which the traditional educator can't. . .

Paulo Freire: . . .and also what some new pedagogies also can't manage to do as they exaggerate the happiness, the affective element, to the detriment of cognitive development.

Moacir Gadotti: I think that traditional pedagogy wasn't able to see this since it was only at the beginning of this century that the educational sciences developed and showed to what extent the affective helps to determine the cognitive.

Traditional pedagogy doesn't have the resources of knowledge that have been developed from the New School pedagogy: the act of knowing is as natural as the act of walking, feeding, loving, etc. Because of this, the affective was dissociated from the cognitive. . .

Paulo Freire: It certainly was, and the result was that it used discipline far too much. As the act of learning became something which was more or less outside his normal life, it became necessary to discipline the pupil so that he could learn. Evidently, without dichotomizing, the act of studying has demanded, ever since it began, a discipline which is an integral part of it, a discipline which puts it into motion without which the pupil cannot study. However, this discipline is in no way a discipline that martyrizes. This must be made clear.

Moacir Gadotti: Exactly. The dilemma of the school, and of education in general, has been this: that of organically and dialectically combining freedom and discipline, freedom and authority.

On one hand, the traditional school is too centered on discipline. On the other hand, the New School is too centered on freedom. In addition, there is the socialist school (we can provisionally call it this, but it could have another name), which stands out as a synthesis of the two main types of school in the years before the third millennium, which we want to see as something new. In the socialist school, freedom and discipline are not mechanically opposed; they are dialectically united through a combination of opposites.

Paulo, to end with a slightly personal question: what do you want to do at this end of the century? What are your present and future projects?

Paulo Freire: This is a question you should make and I'm going to give you a simple answer although it's not a brilliant one. It's a reply that I should make for the sixteen- to twenty-year-olds for whom you are writing. I don't really know what to tell you about what I'm going to do, what I'm planning, but one thing I'll make clear is that I like the question as my reply is that I have no intention of retiring.

I'm now more than seventy, and at the end of century, in whose final moment I hope to take part—maybe giving an interview to a television channel, or drinking *cachaça* or a good wine—I'm sure I'll be committed, as much as I am today, to a bohemian pedagogy of happiness, in the way that I am, tropical. This will be a pedagogy of laughter, of questioning, of curiosity, of seeing the future through the present, a pedagogy that believes in the possibility of the transformation of the world, that believes in history as a possibility.

Notes

Foreword

1. Margaret E. Keck. *The Workers' Party and Democratization in Brazil.* (New Haven and London, Yale University Press, 1992), pages, 61–94.

2. See the following books of Moacir Gadotti: *L'éducation contre l'éducation: l'oubli de l'éducation au travers de l'education permanente* (Lausanne, L' Age d' Homme, 1979); *Educação e poder: Introdução à pedagogia do conflito* (São Paulo, Editora Autores Associados e Editora Cortez, 1980); *Concepção Dialética da educação: Um estudo introdutório* (São Paulo, Cortez Editora-Editora Autores Associados, 1983); *Dialética do amor paterno* (São Paulo, Cortez Editora-Editora Autores Associados, 1985); *Educação e compromisso* (Campinas, Papirus, 1985); with Paulo Freire and Sérgio Guimarães, *Pedagogía: Diálogo e donflito* (São Paulo, Cortez Editora, 1985); *Comunicação docente* (São Paulo, Loyola, 1975); *Pensamento pedagógico Brasileiro* (São Paulo, Ática, 1988), *Marx: Transformar o mundo* (São Paulo, FTD, 1989); *Una só escola para todos: caminbos da autonomia escolar* (Petrópolis, Vozes, 1990); *Escola cidadã* (São Paulo, Cortez Editora-Editora Autores Associados, 1992); *História das idéias pedagógicas* (São Paulo, Ática, 1993); Moacir Gadotti and José Eustáquio Romão (editors), *Município c educação* (São Paulo, Cortez Editora, 1993). The translation of this book is from a revised and updated version of the original in Portuguese entitled *Convite a Leitura de Paulo Freire* (São Paulo, Scipione, 1988).

Introduction

1. Paulo Freire, *La pedagogia degli opressi* (Milano, Arnoldo Mondadori, 1971), p. 11.

2. *Gli intellettuali e l'organizazione della cultura.*

3. Roger Garaudy. "A pedagogia de Paulo Freire e os teólogos da libertação," in *O ocidente é um acidente: por um diálogo das civilizações.*

4. Larry Rother, "Radical Theorist Takes His Message to the World." *New York Times,* 19 August 1986.

Chapter 1. We Can Also Learn in the Shade of the Mangoes

1. *Sobre educação: diálogos,* p. 19.

2. Ibid., p. 92.

3. Essa escola chamada vida, p. 7.

4. Catholic Action: an organization set up by the Catholic Church in the 1920s to publicize Catholicism. It was formed by grassroots teams, diocesan, regional, and national federations and national councils. In the 1950s this group had an important role in the formation and organization of in the struggle for grassroots reforms.

5. From his preface to *A igreja dos oprimidos* edited by Helena Salem.

6. Interview in the newspaper *Pasquin* (Rio de Janeiro, Brazil), 5 May 1978.

7. After a difficult period of recovery, Paulo Freire found love again at the age of sixty-six with Ana Maria A. Hasche, an ex-pupil, to whom he had given the secondary school admission exam in Recife when he was a young teacher. She was a fifty-four-year-old widow. They were married on August 19th, 1988.

8. *Medo e ousadia: o cotidiano do professor*, p. 40.

9. Paulo Freire, *Essa escola chamada vida*, p. 8.

10. Jean Piaget (1896–1980), Swiss psychologist famous for his research on the intelligence of children.

11. MCP (Movement for Popular Culture) was the idea of Miguel Arraes, elected mayor of Recife in 1958. It consisted of the setting up of schools for the people, using rooms belong to neighborhood associations, sports clubs, and religous buildings. In 1960 just adult literacy schemes were working. In the following year, the Catholic Church set up the MEB—the Movement for Grassroots Education, which would involve not just literacy schemes but also schemes to bring awareness and to raise the cultural level of the mass of population, and thereby rescuing the essential connection between education and culture. From the time of its foundation, Paulo Freire participated in the MCP and elaborated his literacy method as part of the movement.

12. *Medo e ousadia: o cotidiano do professor*, p. 31.

13. In Márcio Moreira Alves, O Cristo do povo, p. 13.

14. Celso de Rui Beisiegel, *Poltica e educação popular: a teoria e a prática de Paulo Freire no Brasil*, p. 24.

15. ISEB (Higher Institute for Brazilian Studies), set up by President Juscelino Kubitschek in July 1955, was closed down in April 1965 after the military coup. It comprised intellectuals who attempted to spread the social sciences as an instrument of analysis and of the critical understanding of the Brazilian situation. Important names are Álvaro Vieira Pinto, Hélio Jaguaribe, Nelson Werneck Sodré and Roland Corbisier. "Isebism" was characterized by the value it gave to the role of conscience and of ideology in Brazilian development. It attempted to construct a nonalienating Brazilian conscience. Left-wing critics of "isebism" tried to show its "liberal" presuppositions, that is, the "class alliance" that would be needed for national development.

16. *Pedagogia: diálogo e conflito*, p. 32.

17. Social democracy: a political doctrine of socialist movements which accepts that liberal democratic movements, the market economy, and private property are able to generate a gradual socialization of goods and achieve a relative equality between people. Social democrats renounce both the construction of an egalitarian socialist society and the path of socialism through revolution.

18. In a text published in *Revista Brasileira de Estudos Pedagógicos* in 1961.

19. Ibid.

20. "Banking education" is the type of education which considers the pupils to be empty containers, into which the the teacher will "pour" knowledge.

21. Taken from a text written by Paulo Freire, 1968, Chile, for a seminar about education and agrarian reform.

22. *Medo e ousadia: o cotidiano do professor*, pp. 18–19.

Chapter 2. The Method Which Took Paulo Freire into Exile

1. This explanation is mostly based on two works: *Tecnologia, educação e democracia* by Lauro de Oliveira Lima, and *O que é método Paulo Freire* by Carlos Rodrigues Brandão. I must add that the development of the method which is presented here is no more than a possibility as, in Paulo Freire's proposal (a dialectical method), there is no rigid and inflexible sequence or methodological absolutes.

2. Humanization is the way in which men and women can become aware of themselves, their way of behaving and of thinking, when they develop all their capacities by thinking not just of themselves but of the needs of everyone.

3. In a dialogue with Frei Betto in the book *Essa escola chamada vida*, pp. 14–15.

4. Paulo Freire distinguishes three levels of conscience: the ingenuous conscience, the critical conscience, and the conscience in transit. These range from the conscience in its natural state to the form it takes on when it is fully able to reveal reality. These are not formal levels, neither in terms of content nor in terms of operationalization.

5. Taken out of the daily universe of the literacy student, the *generative word* should generate other words that will allow a reading of reality that is not just linguistic but also political.

The *cultural circle* is a teaching unit that replaces the traditional school. It is formed by a group of people who get together to discuss their work, local and national realities, their family life, etc. There is no place for the traditional (banking) teacher—the one who knows everything—nor is there for the pupil who knows nothing. The cultural circle allows the pupil to, at the same time as he becomes literate, to learn to "read," that is, analyze his practice and act upon it.

6. *Codification*: the representation of a situation lived by the student in his daily work. This is related to the generative word. It includes certain aspects of the problem which is being studied and provides some examples of concrete text.

Decodification is one of the most important moments in the process of alphabetization. It is the analysis of the generative words (or linguistic code) to extract the existential elements which are contained in it.

7. This example is taken from a mimeographed document for the cultural circles of Mossoró and Angicos (1961–62) and quoted by Carlos Rodrigues Brandão in *O que é método Paulo Freire*, pp. 53–54.

8. Celso de Rui Beisiegel, "Cultura do povo e educação popular," in Edênio Valle and José J. Queiroz, eds., *A cultura do povo* 3d. ed. (São Paulo: Cortez, 1985), pp. 53–54.

9. *Hominization*: the evolutionary stage of the world when man and woman appeared; in other words, when the capacity to reflect and act on reality in order to transform it appeared.

Conscientization is a word that is used by Freire (and distorted by many people) to show the relationship that should exist between thinking and acting. A person (or better, a group of people) who become conscientized (without forgetting that no one conscientizes anyone else, but that people are conscientized mutually, through their daily work) is able to discover the reason why things are the way they are. This discovery should be accompanied by a transforming action.

Praxis is the unity that should exist between what one does (practice) and what one thinks about what one does (theory). A common concept in Marxism, which is also called philosophy of praxis, it designates the reaction of man to his real conditions of existence, his capacity to insert himself in production (productive praxis) and in the transformation of society (revolutionary praxis).

10. *Vozes* (Petrópolis, Rio de Janeiro) 79 (Jan./Feb. 1981).

11. The book *A paixão de conhecer o mundo*, by Madalena Freire, contains her experience in the schools Escola Criarte and Escola da Vila in São Paulo between 1978 and 1981 and is based on the ideas that the child is the subject of the educational process and that there is no dichotomy between the cognitive and affective aspects but rather a dynamic and pleasurable relationship between them which is directed towards diiscovering the world. In interviews she gave to to educator Fanny Abramovich, Ms. Freire admits that she learned the importance of the association between doing and knowing from her father.

Chapter 3. Learning from History

1. USAID—the United States Agency for International Development—was the executive organ of the policy which had been set by the Alliance for Progress to modernize the educational systems of the countries of the so-called Third

World. It made a large number of agreements and technical cooperation links with the Ministry of Education and Culture, the MEC-USAID programs, especially in the sixties, when the U.S. was exporting reforms that had taken place in the twenties and which had been designed to preserve the structure behind a democratic façade with equality of opportunities and technical-financial cooperation.

2. Alliance for Progress: An organ created by the U.S. with the supposed aim of helping the peoples of Latin America. In 1961, President John Kennedy said that, with this help, Latin America could, in ten years, solve its basic developmental problems by borrowing money from rich countries. Its motto was "Progress with Freedom." As could be forecast, the result was the enormous debt of the countries that adhered to this "alliance."

3. *Aprendendo com a própria história*, p. 41.

4. Ibid.

5. Guillermo Willianson C., "Paulo Freire: 1965–1969. Su paso por Chile y el Chile por que pasó."

6. Cultural invasion is the penetration in a given society of a foreign culture that invades it and imposes on it its way of being and seeing the world.

7. PAIGC—Partido Africano para a Independência da Guinea-Bissau e Cabo Verde (African Party for the Independence of Guinea-Bissau and Cabo Verde). MPLA—Movimento Popular de Libertação de Angola (Popular Movement for the Liberation of Angola). FRELIMO—Frente de Libertação de Moçambique (Mozambique Liberation Front).

8. *Por uma pedagogia da pergunta*, p. 20–21.

9. Published in Spanish by ICIRA in 1969. It was translated into Portuguese by Rosiska Darcy de Oliveira and published in 1971.

10. First published in English and Spanish in 1970. It was only published in Brazil four years later, although it had been written in 1968. *Pedagogy of the Oppressed* was translated into seventeen languages and the preface was done by Ernani Maria Fiori. Freire's books have been published in many different languages and have influenced a whole generation of educators and political militants.

11. Published in 1970 in the *Harvard Education Review* as an essay, and in 1972 with a preface by João da Veiga Coutinho by Penguin in Britain. The Portuguese version, which included other essays, was only printed in 1976.

12. Amílcar Cabral, leader of PAIGC, an "educator educating his people," according to Paulo Freire in the dedication to *Cartas à Guiné Bissau*, the hero of the people and friend of all, was assassinated in 1973, seven months before the proclamation of independence of Guinea-Bissau.

Chapter 4. A Pedagogy for Libertion

1. From a lecture given on the opening of the first public session of the Forum of Education of São Paulo state, August 1983.

2. In the journal *Paz e terra* (Rio de Janeiro) 9.

3. *Sobre educação*, pp. 77–78.

4. Paulo Freire thinks it's much more comfortable for an educator to be authoritarian, since predominance doesn't demand competence or respect and it exempts explanations.

5. *Pedagogia: diálogo e conflito*, p. 76.

6. Paulo Freire and Ira Shor, *Medo e ousadia: o cotidiano do professor*, pp. 203–4.

7. Ibid.

8. "A alfabetização de adultos: é ela um quefazer neutro?" p. 70.

9. *Por uma pedagogia da pergunta*, p. 38.

10. Ibid., p. 56.

11. *Pedagogia: diálogo e conflito*, p. 123.

12. In *A mensagem de Paulo Freire: teoria e prática da libertação* (The Message of Paulo Freire: Theory and Practice of Liberation). Texts selected by INODEP (Porto: Nova Crítica, 1977), p. 33.

13. Diana A. Cunha, *As utopias da educação; ensaios sobre as propostas de Paulo Freire*, pp. 28–29.

Chapter 5. Relearning Brazil

1. Paulo Freire, "Debate com os professores mineiros."

2. Paulo Freire, Moacir Gadotti, and Sérgio Guimarães, *Pedagogia: diálogo e conflito*, pp. 56–57.

3. *Sobre educação dialogo*, pp. 14–15.

4. Ibid., p. 83.

5. This book was classified among the five best publications on the subject by the American Reading Association.

6. *Concepção dialética da história*, pp. 13–14.

Chapter 6. A Revolutionary Educator

1. Paulo Freire at the Congress of the Brazilian Christian Union of Social Communication, Methodist University of São Bernardo, Greater São Paulo, November 1980.

2. *Pedagogia do oprimido*, p. 45.

3. Interview in *Vozes* (Petrópolis) 59 (Jan./Feb. 1982).

4. Interview in *Interação* (São Paulo) 4 (Jun./Jul. 1984).

5. *Diário da Assembléia Nacional Constituinte*, 21 July 1987. I Year, no. 100 (supplement), *Atas das Comissões* (Brasília), p. 226.

6. See "Paulo Freire como administrador público" a preface by Moacir Gadotti and Carlos Alberto Torres to *A educação na cidade*, Paulo Freire's book. See also Carlos Alberto Torres, *The State, Social Movements and Educational Policies in Latin America: A Study of Municipal Policies in São Paulo, Brazil* (UCLA: Los Angeles, Research Plan, 1992).

7. *A educação na cidade*, p. 22.

8. Ibid., p. 79.

9. Ibid., p. 80.

10. Ibid., p. 80.

11. See Maria José Vale Ferreira, *Princípios político-pedagógicos do MOVA-SP*, São Paulo, MOVA-SP, Caderno no. 3, Secretaria Municipal de Educação (July 1990).

12. See Moacir Gadotti and Carlos Alberto Torres, *Estado e educação popular na América Latina*.

13. See Moacir Gadotti, *Escola cidadã*.

14. *A educação na cidade*, P. 143.

15. Ibid., p. 144.

Chapter 7. Paulo Freire in the Context of Contemporary Pedagogical Thought

1. A progressive conception of theology and of the social and political role of the church. It has developed especially in Latin America and defends the involvement of Christians in

the struggle for liberation. It is opposed to dogmatic theology, which establishes a rigid code of conduct for Christians, based on the defense of tradition, family, and property. Liberation theology uses the dialectic method to analyze reality.

2. French socialist educator, who, while a primary school teacher, developed an important struggle against the bureaucratized pedagogy and the authoritarianism of traditional education. He introduced new pedagogical techniques such as the free text and printing. Paulo Freire exchanged letters and didactic material with the French association of Frenetian educators.

3. French philosopher who wrote a treatise on education, describing what course the education of a boy should take from birth to the age of twenty-five. This boy, a fictional character, was given the name of Émile, title of Rousseau's main work.

4. American psychotherapist who extended his methods and ideas on reeducation to the area of pedagogy. He believed that an atmosphere of freedom of experience and a teaching centered on the student would help his complete development as each individual has his own resources to develop as long as he is in a free atmosphere.

5. Born in Vienna in 1926, Ivan Illich was a priest for a number of years in Austria and Italy. After working in New York, he directed the Catholic University of Puerto Rico and founded in Cuernavaca, Mexico, CIDOC, an intercultural center of documentation, where one could learn Spanish, get to know the Latin American, world and take part in the critical analysis of industrial society.

6. *La cuestión escolar*, p. 647.

7. Anísio Spínola Teixeira (1900–71), a well-known educator from Bahia in Brazil, a defender of liberal education and the public school. He introduced the thinking of John Dewey into Brazil, in the defense of the New School. A thinker,

statesman, and man of action, he was one of the founders of the University of Brasília. *Educação não é privilégio* (Education is Not a Privilege), published in 1957, in which he defends the democratization of teaching, is his most famous work.

8. *Harvard Educational Review* 47, no. 3 (August 1977).

9. Anton Makarenko (1888–1939), revolutionary Soviet educator, who researched the fundamental principles of collective education, putting it into practice in the Gorky Colony with abandoned children, and in the Dzerjínski Commune. He gave special emphasis to the link between education and production. Among his works is *Pedagogic Poem*.

10. Revolutionary educator who set up the so-called School of Work, conceiving it as an instrument for the self-organization of the pupils, based on the study of the relationships of man with contemporary reality. Knowledge of the real and self-organization are the fundamental elements with which the school can contribute to the establishment of new social relationships, based on equality and solidarity.

11. Emmanuel Mounier (1905–50), French Christian philosopher who attempted to maintain a dialogue between atheists and communists. He founded an ethicopolitical doctrine called personalism, which said that the value of the person was above everything else. Personalism is different from individualism, which weakens the value of solidarity, and is a long way from collectivism, which puts the collective interest above everything else.

12. Rosiska Darcy de Oliveira and Pierre Dominicé, *Freire versus Illich*, p. 33.

Conclusion

1. "Journée rencontre avec Paulo Freire," INFREP (Institut National de Formation et Recherche en Education Permanente), Convention Center "La Villette," Paris, December 12, 1991.

2. Paulo Freire often makes reference to Marx's speech: "I am not Marxist!"

3. Interview in *Folha de São Paulo*, newspaper of São Paulo City, 17 April 1992.

4. Moacir Gadotti, *Escola vivida, escola projetada*

5. This respect, despite small theoretical divergencies, can be demonstrated by the fact that Paulo Freire trusted me with the task of establishing an Institute, which emerged from an idea of his on April 12, 1991, at the University of California, Los Angeles, on the occasion of his visit to this university. The Paulo Freire Institute is already setting up a network of more than fifty scholars of the thought of this great Brazilian educator throughout the world. By means of the critical and systematic study, of research and documentation, training and information with regard to his thought and that of others, the Paulo Freire Institute aims to maintain Paulo Freire's legacy alive and active.

6. Paulo Freire is publishing a rereading of the *Pedagogy of the Oppressed* twenty four years after its first publication, telling the story of the book and making new announcements, within the context of education at the close of this century. Freire's new book has as its title, *Pedagogy of Hope*.

Bibliography

I. Paulo Freire's Main Works (in Chronological Order)

"A educação de adultos e as populações marginais. O problema dos mocambos" (Adult education and marginal populations). Seminário Regional Preparatório em Pernambuco; in *Anais do II Congresso Nacional de Educação de Adultos* (Annals of the 2nd National Congress of Adult Education), Rio de Janeiro: Ministério da Educação e Cultura, 1958.

Educação e atualidade brasileira (Education and the Brazilian present). Recife: Universidade Federal de Recife, 1959.

"Escola primária para o Brasil" (Primary Education for Brazil). *Revista Brasileira de estudos Pedagógicos*. (Rio de Janeiro, INEP-MEC) 35 (82) (Apr./Jun. 1961), pp. 15–33.

"Conscientização e alfabetização; uma nova visão do precesso" (Concientization and literacy; a new vision of the process). *Estudos Universitários*. (Recife) 5 (Apr./Jun. 1963), pp. 5–23.

Educação como prática da liberdade (Education as a practice of freedom). Rio de Janeiro: Paz e Terra, 1967.

The Cultural Action Process: An Introduction to its Understanding. Cambridge, Mass.: Center for Studies in Education and Development, Graduate School of Education, Harvard University, October 1969.

Adult Education as Cultural Action. Cambridge, Mass.: Center for Studies in Education and Development, Graduate School of Education, Harvard University, October 1969.

"Witness to liberation." In *Seeing Education Whole*. Geneva: WCC, 1970. With Tom Paxton, Jacques Prevert, Charles Hurst, Martin Conway, and Ellis Nelson.

"Papel da educação na humanização" (The role of communication in humanization). *Revista Paz e Terra*. Rio de Janeiro: Paz e Terra, 1971.

Extensão ou comunicação? (Extension or communication?) Rio de Janeiro: Paz e Terra, 1971.

Pedagogia do oprimido (Pedagogy of the oppressed). Rio de Janeiro: Paz e Terra, 1974.

Educación para el cambio social (Education for social change). Buenos Aires: Tierra Nueva, 1974.

Diálogo: descolarización, estruturas, liberaciones, educación (Dialog: Deschooling, structure, liberation, education). Buenos Aires: Busqueta/Celadec, 1975. With Ivan Illich.

Ação cultural para a liberdade e outros escritos (Cultural action for freedom and other writings). Rio de Janeiro: Paz e Terra, 1976.

"A alfabetização de adultos: é ela um quefazer neutro?" (Adult literacy: Is it a neutral task?). *Educação & sociedade* (Campinas) 1(1) (Sept. 1978), pp. 64–70.

Os cristãos e a libertação dos oprimidos (The Christians and the freedom of the oppressed). Lisbon: Edições BASE, 1978.

Education for Critical Consciousness. New York: Seabury Press, 1978.

"Terceiro mundo e teologia. Carta a um jovem teólogo" (The Third World and Theology). In Carlos Alberto Torres, *Consciência e história: a praxis educativa da Paulo Freire* (Consciousness and History: The Educative Praxis of Paulo Freire) São Paulo: Loyola, 1979.

Conscientização: teoria e prática da libertação (Conscientization: Theory and practice of freedom). São Paulo: Cortez & Moraes, 1979.

Edução e mundança (Education and change). Rio de Janeiro: Paz e Terra, 1979.

"Exílio e identidade: a tragetória de anos do IDAC" (Exile and identity: The trajetory of the IDAC years). In Paulo Freire, Claudius Ceccon, Miguel Darcy de Oliveira, and Rojiska Darcy de Oliverira, *Vivendo e aprendendo: experiências do IDAC em educação*, pp. 9–14. São Paulo: Brasiliense, 1980.

"Quatro cartas aos animadores de círculos de cultura de São Tomé e Príncipe" (Four letters to the animators of the cultural circles of São Tomé and Príncipe). In Carlos Rodrigues Brandão, *A questão política da educação popular* (The Political Question of popular education), pp. 136–95. São Paulo: Brasiliense, 1980.

"The People Speak Their Word: Learning to Read and Write in São Tomé and Príncipe". Translated by Loretta Slover. *Harvard Educational Review* I (51) (February 1981), pp. 27–30.

Der Lehrer ist Politiker und Künstler. Hamburg: Rowohlt Taschenbuch Verlag, 1981. Edited by Birgit Wingenroth.

Cartas à Guiné-Bissau. Registros de uma experiência em processo (Letters to Guinéa-Bissau. Registering an experience in Process). Rio de Janeiro: Paz e Terra, 1981.

Ideologia e educação: reflexões sobre a não neutralidade da educação (Ideology and education: Reflections on the non-neutrality of education). Rio de Janeiro: Paz e Terra, 1981.

"Criando métodos de pesquisa e alternativas: aprendendo a fazer melhor através da ação" (Creating methods of research and alternatives: Learning how to do better through action). In Carlos Rodrigues Brandão, *Pesquisa participante* (Participatory research). São Paulo: Brasiliense, 1981.

"Debate com os professores mineiros" (Debate with teachers of Minas Gerais). Belo Horizonte, April 1981. Mimeo.

A importância do ato de ler em três artigos que se completam (The importance of reading in three articles that complement each other). São Paulo: Cortez/Autores Associados, 1982.

"Educação: o sonho possível" (Education: A possible dream). In Carlos Rodrigues Brandão, *O educador: vida e morte* (The educator: Life and death), pp. 81–101. Rio de Janeiro, Graal: 1982.

Paulo Freire ao vivo (Paulo Freire alive). São Paulo: Loyola, 1983. With Aldo Vannucchi and Wlademir dos Santos.

Sobre educação: diálogos (On education: Dialogues). Rio de Janeiro: Paz e Terra, vol. 1, 1982 and vol. 2, 1984. With Séergio Guimarães.

"O sentido da avaliação na prática da base" (The meaning of assessment on grassroots practice). In José J. Queiróz, *A educação popular nas comunidades eclesiais de base* (Popular education in the grassroots communities of the church), pp. 97–101. São Paulo: Paulinas, 1985.

Essa escola chamada vida (This school called life). São Paulo: Atica, 1985. With Frei Betto.

Por uma pedagogia da pergunta (Learning to question: A pedagogy of liberation. Geneva: WCC Publications, 1989). Rio de Janeiro: Paz e Terra, 1985. With Antonio Faundez.

Pedagogia: diálogo e conflito (Pedagogy: dialogue and conflict). São Paulo: Cortez, 1985. With Moacir Gadotti and Sérgio Guimarães.

The Politics of Education: Culture, Power and Liberation. South Hadley, Mass.: Bergin & Garvey, 1985. Introduction by Henry A. Giroux and translated by Donaldo Macedo.

Fazer escola conhecendo a vida (Building a school knowing life). Campinas: Papirus, 1986. With Adriano Nogueira and Débora Mazza.

Aprendendo com a própria história (Learning with one's own history). Rio de Janeiro: Paz e Terra, 1987. With Sérgio Guimarães.

"A alfabetização como elemento da formação da cidadania" (Literacy as an element of training for citizenship). Brasília, May 1987.

Medo e ousadia: o cotidiano do professor (Pedagogy for liberation: Dialogues on transforming education. South Hadley, Mass.: Bergin & Garvey, 1987). Rio de Janeiro: Paz e Terra, 1987. With Ira Shor.

Literacy: Reading the Word and the World. South Hadley, Mass.: Bergin & Garvey, 1987. With Donaldo Macedo.

Na escola que fazemos. . .uma relação interdisciplinar em educação popular (It is at school that we do. . .an interdisciplinary relationship on popular education). Petrópolis: Vozes, 1988. Edited by Adriano Nogueira and Débora Mazza.

Educadores de rua; uma abordagem crtica (Street educators: A critical approach). Brasília: Unicef, 1989.

Conversando con educadores (Talking with educators). Montevideo: Roca Viva, 1990.

We Make the Road by Walking: Conversations on Education and Social Change. Philadelphia: Temple University Press, 1990. Edited by Brenda Bell, John Gaventa, and John Peters. With Myles Horton.

A educação na cidade (Education in the city). São Paulo: Cortez, 1991.

II. Main Works about Paulo Freire and Other Consulted Works

Abramovich, Fanny. *Quem educa quem?* (Who educates who?). São Paulo: Summus, 1985.

"Alfabetização em 40 horas: Goulart fala em Angicos" (Literacy in 40 hours: Goulart talks in Angicos). *Folha de São Paulo,* 3 March 1963.

"A liberdade em aula" (Freedom in the classroom). *Interação* 1(4):35 (Jun./Jul. 1984), p. 6.

Alves, Márcio Moreira. *O Cristo do povo* (Christ of the people). Rio de Janeiro: Sabiá, 1968.

Apple, Michael W. *Ideology and Curriculum.* London: Routledge and Kegan Paul, 1979.

Aronowitz, Stanley, and Henry A. Giroux. *Postmodern Education: Politics, Culture, and Social Criticism.* Minneapolis: University of Minnessota Press, 1991.

Assman, Hugo. *Opressión-liberación: desafio a los cristianos* (Oppression-liberation: A challenge to Christians). Montevideo: Tierra Nueva, 1971.

Aukerman, Robert C. *Approaches to Beginning Reading.* New York: John Wiley, 1971.

Avalone Filho, Olavo. "Paulo Freire, o educador do povo. Quem é ele e o que pensa?" (Paulo Freire, popular educator. Who is he and what does he think?). *Folha de São Paulo,* 12 November 1978, p. 50.

Azevedo, Licínio, and Rodrigues, Maria da Paz. "Diário da libertação" (Diary of liberation). *Versus* (São Paulo 1977).

Baron, S., et al. *Unpopular Education.* London: Hutchinson & Co., 1981.

Barros, Helene. "A experiência de aplicação do método Paulo Freire na alfabetização de adultos em Brasilia" (The experience of tryng Paulo Freire's method in adult's literacy in Brasilia). In *Paulo Freire e a educação brasileira* (Paulo Freire and Brazilian education), pp. 6–11. Brasília: Frente Cultural de Brasília, 1982.

Beisiegel, Celso de Rui. "O método Paulo Freire de alfabetização de adultos" (Paulo Freire's methods of adult literacy). In *Estado e educação popular: um estudo sobre a educação* (The state and popular education: A study on education), pp. 164–72. São Paulo: Pioneira, 1974.

_____. *Política e educação popular* a teoria e a practica de Paulo Freire no Brasil (Politics and popular education). São Paulo: Ática, 1982.

Bellanova, Bartolomeo. *Paulo Freire: educazione problematizzante e prassi sociale per la liberazione* (Paulo Freire: Questioning education and social practice for liberation). Bologna: Centro Programmazione, 1978.

Belotti, Elena Gianini. *Little Girls.* London: Writers and Readers, 1976.

Bendit, René, and Achim Heimbucher. *Von Paulo Freire lernen.* Munich: Juventa Verlag, 1979.

Berggren, Carol and Lars Berggren. *The Literacy Process: A Practice in Domestication or Liberation.* London: Writers and Readers, 1975.

Borda, Orlando Fals. *Conocimiento y poder popular: lecciones con campesinos de Nicaragua, Mexico y Colombia* (Knowledge and popular power: Lessons with the "campesinos" of Nicaragua, Mexico and Colombia). Mexico City: Siglo Vientiuno, 1986.

_____, ed. *A questão política da educação popular* (The political question of popular education). São Paulo: Brasiliense, 1980.

_____, ed. *O educador: vida e morte* (The educator: Life and death). Rio de Janeiro: Graal, 1982.

Brandão, Carlos Rodrigues, *O que é método Paulo Freire* (What Paulo Freire's method is). São Paulo: Brasiliense, 1981.

Britto, Jomard Muniz de. "Educação de adultos e unificação da cultura" (Adult education and cultural unification). *Estudos Universitários* (cultural review of the University of Recife) (Apr./Jun. 1983), pp. 61–70.

Brown, Cynthia. *Literacy in 30 Hours: Paulo Freire's Process in Northeast Brazil.* Chicago: Alternate Schools Network, 1975.

Cabral, Amílcar. *Obras escolhidas de Amilcar Cabral.* 2 vols. (Amilcar Cabral's selected works). Lisbon: Seara Nova, 1977.

"Caminhos de Paulo Freire" (The paths of Paulo Freire), *Ensaio* (São Paulo) 14 (1985), pp. 1–27. Interview with J. Chasin, Rui Gomes Dantas, and Vicente Madeira.

Carnoy, Martin. *Education as Cultural Imperialism.* New York: David McKay, 1974.

Carnoy, Martin, and Henry M. Levin. *Schooling and Work in the Democratic State.* Stanford: Stanford University Press, 1985.

Carnoy, Martin, and Joel Samoff, eds. *Education and Social Transition in the Third World.* Princeton: Princeton University Press, 1990.

Cavalcanti, Paulo. *O caso eu conto como o caso foi* (The case I'll tell you what the case was like). Recife: Guararapos, 1979.

Cintra, Eliseu. "O sentido do outro em Paulo Freire" (The sense of the other in Paulo Freire). M.A. dissertation (Tese de Mestrado, Pontifícia Universidade Católica de São Paulo, 1986.

Coimbra, Osvaldo. "Paulo Freire: Não sou contra as cartilhas de alfabetização" (I'm not against literacy primers). *Nova escola* 1(3) (Apr. 1986), pp. 48–50.

Collins, Denis E. *Two Utopians: A Comparison and Contrast of the Educational Philosophies of Paulo Freire and Theodore Brameld.* Berkeley: Department of Education, University of Southern California, 1973.

_____. *Paulo Freire: his Life, Works and Thought.* New York: Paulist Press, 1977.

Cunha, Diana A. *As utopias da educação; ensaios sobre as propostas de Paulo Freire* (The utopia of education: Essays on Paulo Freire's proposals). Rio de Janeiro: Paz e Terra, 1985.

Dewey, John. *Democracy and Education.* New York: Free Press, 1966.

Elias, John Lawrence. *Conscientization and Deschooling: Freire and Illich's Proposals for Reshaping Society.* Philadelphia: Westminister Press, 1976.

"Entrevista com Paulo Freire" (An Interview with Paulo Freire). *Folha de São Paulo* (São Paulo daily newspaper) 26 August 1979, pp. 3–7.

"Este é Paulo Freire" (This is Paulo Freire). *Versus* (São Paulo) 2(13) (August 1977), pp. 38–39. Debate between Paulo Freire and Ivan Illich.

"Encontro com Paulo Freire" (A meeting with Paulo Freire). *Educação & sociedade* (Campinas, SP) 1(3) (May 1979), pp. 47–75. Interview with Lígia Chiappini Moraes Leite.

Fanon, Frantz. *The Wretched of the Earth.* New York: Grove Press, 1965.

Faria, Wilson de. "O ensino Libertário" (The libertarian teaching). In *Teorias de ensino e planejamento pedagógico* (Teaching Theories and Pedagogic Plan), pp. 27–50. São Paulo: EPU, 1987.

Faundez, Antonio. "Notas sobre a cultura escrita e o processo da alfabetização nas ilhas de São Tomé e Príncipe" (Notes on written culture and alphabetization in the islands of São Tomé and Príncipe). *Educação & Sociedade* (São Paulo, Cortez/CEDES) 6(19) (August 1984), pp. 73–90.

_____. *Oralité et écriture en Afrique* (Oral culture and writing in Africa). Geneva: World Council of Churches, 1986.

Favero, Osmar, ed. *Cultura popular; educação popular. memórias dos anos 60* (Popular culture; popular education. Memories of the sixties). Rio de Janeiro: Graal, 1983.

Ferreiro, Emília, and Teberrosky, Ana. *Psicogênese da lngua escrita* (The psychogenesis of written language). Porto Alegre: Artes Médicas, 1986.

Fleuri, Reinaldo Matias, ed. *Educar para quê? Contra o autoritarismo da relação pedagógica na escola* (What to educate for? Against the authoritarianism of the pedagogical relationship at school). Uberlândia, UFUB-MG, Goiânia, UCG-GO, 1986.

François, Marie-Louise. *Referat auf der Tatung Paulo Freires Methode der Bewubtseigsbildung.* Huy, Belgium: Friedens-akademie Tihange, Université de la Paix, 1974.

Freinet, Célestin. *A educação pelo trabalho* (Education through work). Lisbon, Presença, 1974.

Freire, Madalena. *A paixão de conhecer o mundo* (Passion to know the world). Rio de Janeiro: Paz e Terra, 1983.

Furter, Pierre. "Paulo Freire ou o poder da palavra" (Paulo Freire or the word's power). In Paulo Freire *Educação como prática da liberdade* (Education as a practice of freedom). Rio de Janeiro: Paz e Terra, 1967.

Gadotti, Moacir. *A educação contra a educação* (Education against education). Rio de Janeiro: Paz e Terra, 1981.

_____. "É possível aplicar o método Paulo Freire hoje?" (Is it possible to apply Paulo Freire's method today?) In *Educação e compromisso* (Education and commitment), pp. 45–49. Campinas: Papirus, 1985.

_____. "A educação como ato poltico: a "Pedagogia do oprimido" (Education as a political act: The "pedagogy of the oppressed"). In *Pensamento pedagógico brasileiro* (Brasilian pedagogical thinking), pp. 26–38. São Paulo: Ática, 1987.

_____. *Escola cidadã* (Citizen school). São Paulo: Cortez, 1992.

_____. *Escola vivida, escola projetada* (Lived school, projected school). Campinas: Papirus, 1992.

Gadotti, Moacir, and Carlos Alberto Torres. *Estado e educação popular na América Latina* (State and popular education in Latin America). Campinas: Papirus, 1992.

Gajardo, Marcela. *La Concientizacion en America Latina: una revision critica* (Conscientization in Latin America: A critical revision). Mexico City: CREFAL, 1991.

Garaudy, Roger. "A pedagogia de Paulo Freire e os teólogos da libertação" (Paulo Freire's pedagogy and liberation theologians). In *O ocidente è um acidente: por um diálogo das civilizações* (The West is an accident: For a dialogue of civilizations), pp. 141–46. Rio de Janeiro: Salamandra, 1978.

Garcia-Huidobro, Juan Eduardo. "El projecto cultural granisciant." In *Ideas y Valores*, no. 55–56, Bogotá, 1979, pp. 3–42.

Gerhardt, Heinz-Peter. "Angicos: Rio Grande do Norte, 1962/63, a primeira experiência com o sistema Paulo Freire" (Angicos, Rio Grande do Norte state, 1962/63, first experience with Paulo Freire's method). *Educação & sociedade* (São Paulo, Cortez/CEDES) 5(14) (May 1983), pp. 5–34.

Giroux, Henry A. "Paulo Freire and the concept of critical literacy." In *Radical Pedagogy*, pp. 77–82. Philadelphia: Temple University Press, 1982.

———. "Paulo Freire e o conceito de alfabetização crítica" (Paulo Freire and the concept of critical education). In *Pedagogia radical* (Radical pedagogy), pp. 80–87. São Paulo: Cortez/Autores Associados, 1983.

———. *Theory and Resistance in Education: A Pedagogy for Opposition.* South Hadley, Mass.: Bergin & Garvey, 1983.

Giroux, Henry A., and Stanley Aronowitz. *Education under Siege. The Conservative, Liberal and Radical Debate over Schooling.* Amherst, Mass.: Bergin & Garvey, 1984.

Giroux, Henry A., and Peter McLaren eds. *Critical Pedagogy, the State, and Cultural Struggle.* Albany: State University of New York Press, 1989.

Goes, Moacyr de. *De pé no chão também se aprende a ler* (Standing on the floor is also possible to read). Rio de Janeiro: Civilização Brasileira, 1980.

Goulet, Denis. *The Cruel Choice: A New Concept in the Theory of Development.* New York: Atheneum Press, 1971.

_____. *Gli intellettuali e l'organizzazione della cultura* (Intellectuals and the organization of culture). Rome: Guilio Einaudi, 1955.

Gramsci, Antonio. *Concepção dialética da história* (Dialectic conception of history). São Paulo: Civilização Brasileira, 1968.

Guerreiro, Miguel Escobar, ed. *Paulo Freire y la educación liberadora* (Paulo Freire and the liberating education). Mexico City: SEP (Biblioteca Pedagógica), 1985.

_____. *Pedagogia de la comunicación* (Pedagogy of communication). Buenos Aires: Humanitas, 1974.

Gutiérrez, Francisco. *Educación como praxis política* (Education and political practice). Mexico City: Siglo Veintiuno, 1984.

Haddad, Sérgio. "Educação para participação política. O exemplo de Paulo Freire" (Education for political participation. Paulo Freire's example). *Revista de educação AEC* (Brasília) 11(43) (1982), pp. 27–38.

_____. "Conscientização e alfabetização de adultos" (Conscientization and adult literacy). *Cadernos de pesquisa* (São Paulo) 52 (Feb. 1985), pp. 97–100.

Harper, Babete, Claudius Ceccon, Miguel Oliveira, and Rosiska Darcy de Oliveira. *Cuidado, escola!* (School, watch out!) São Paulo: Brasiliense, 1980.

Hernández, Isabel. *Educação e sociedades indígenas; uma aplicação bilíngue do método Paulo Freire* (Education and Indian societies; A bilingual application of Paulo Freire's method). São Paulo: Cortez, 1981.

Hernandez, Isabel, et al. *Saber popular y educación en America Latina* (Popular wisdom and education in Latin America). Buenos Aires: Busqueda, 1985.

Holtz, Harvey, et al., eds. *Education and the American Dream: Conservatives, Liberals and Radicals Debate the Future of Education.* Granby, Mass.: Bergin and Garvey, 1989. Introduction by Paulo Freire and Henry A. Giroux.

Hoyles, Martin, ed. *The Politics of Literacy.* London: Writers and Readers, 1977.

Illich, Ivan. *Deschooling Society.* New York, Harper & Row, 1970.

Jannuzi, Gilberta S. Martino. *Confronto pedagógico: Paulo Freire e Mobral* (Pedagogical confrontation: Paulo Freire and Mobral). São Paulo: Cortez/Moraes, 1979.

Jorge, J. Simões. *A ideologia de Paulo Freire* (Paulo Freire's ideology). São Paulo: Loyola, 1979.

_____. *Sem ódio nem violência; perspectiva da libertação segundo Paulo Freire* (Neither hate nor violence; The perspective of freedom according to Paulo Freire). São Paulo: Loyola, 1979.

_____. *Libertação como alienação? A metodologia antropológica de Paulo Freire* (Freedom as alienation? The anthropological methodology of Paulo Freire). São Paulo: Loyola, 1979.

Kidd, Rody, and Budd Hall, eds. *Adult Learning: A Design for Action.* Oxford: Pergamon Press, 1978.

Kozol, Jonathan. Preface to Paulo Freire, *Pedagogy in Process: The Letters to Guinea-Bissau.* New York: Seabury Press, 1978.

La belle, Thomas J. "Liberation and consciousness raising." In *Non-formal Education and Social Change in Latin America,* pp. 112–26. Los Angeles: UCLA, Latin America Publications, 1975.

Leite, Lígia Chiappini Morals. "Encontro com Paulo Freire" (Meeting with Paulo Freire). *Educação & sociedade* (São Paulo, CEDES/Cortez) 1(3) (May 1979), pp. 47–75.

_____. "Rousseau, Freinet e Paulo Freire: educação transformadora e educação conservadora" (Rousseau, Freinet and Paulo Freire: Transforming education and conservative education). In *Invasão da catedral: literatura e ensino em debate* (Invading cathredal: Literature and teaching debate), pp. 75–77. Porto Alegre: Mercado Aberto, 1983.

Lima, Lauro de Oliveira. "Método Paulo Freire; processo de aceleração da alfabetização de adultos" (Paulo Freire's method; the process of the acceleration of adult literacy). In Oliveira de Lauro, *Tecnologia, educação e democracia* (Rio de Janeiro, Civilização Brasileira), 1979, pp. 173–203.

Lima, Venício Artur de. *Comunicação e cultura: as idéias de Paulo Freire* (Communication and culture: The ideas of Paulo Freire). Rio de Janeiro: Paz e Terra, 1981.

McEoin, Gary. *Revolution Next Door: Latin America in the 1970s.* New York: Rinehart and Winston, 1971.

Mackie, Robert, ed. *Literacy and Revolution: The Pedagogy of Paulo Freire.* New York: Continuum Publishing, 1981. Preface by Jonathan Kozol.

McLaren, Peter. *Life in Schools: An Introduction to Critical Pedagogy in the Foundations of Education.* New York: Longman, 1989.

_____. *Schooling as a Ritual Performance: Towards a Political Economy of Educational Symbols and Gestures.* London: Routledge & Kegan Paul, 1986.

McLaren, Peter, and Peter Leonard, eds. *Paulo Freire: A Critical Encounter; The Compassionate Fire of a Revolutionary Life.* New York: Routledge, 1993. Contributors: Cornel West, Peter McLaren, Stanley Aronowitz, Henry Giroux, Ira Shor, Peter Leonard, Donaldo Macedo, Tomaz Tadeu da Silva, Carlos Alberto Torres, Colin Lankshear, and Paulo Freire.

Makarendo, Anton Semionovitch. *Poema pedagógico* (A pedagogical poem). 3 vols. São Paulo: Brasiliense, 1986.

Manfredi, Sílvia Maria. *Política e educação popular: experiência de alfabetização no Brasil com o método Paulo Freire—1960/1964* (Politics and popular education: A literacy experiment in Brazil with Paulo Freire's method). São Paulo: Cortez/Autores Associados, 1981.

Melo, José Marques de. "A comunicação na pedagogia de Paulo Freire" (Communication in Paulo Freire's pedagogy). In Various, *Comunicação e libertação.* Petrópolis: Vozes, 1981.

Memmi, Albert. *The Colonizer and the Colonized.* Boston: Beacon Press, 1967.

"Método Paulo Freire: um método de conhecimento" (Paulo Freire's method: A method of knowledge). *Folha de São Paulo* 19 November 1978, p. 35.

Monlcús, Antonio. *Pedagogía de la contradicción: Paulo Freire* (Pedagogy of contradiction: Paulo Freire). Barcelona: Anthropos, 1988.

Moura, Manuel. *O pensamento de Paulo Freire: uma revolução na educação* (Paulo Freire's method: A revolution in education). Lisbon: Multinova, 1978.

Musgrave, P., and R. J. Slleck. *Alternative Schools.* Sidney: John Wiley, 1975.

"Não há educação neutra" (There is no neutral education). *Movimento* (São Paulo) 96 (May 1, 1977), pp. 13–14.

Nazario, Julian. "A transformação do mundo: o método Paulo Freire à luz da semiótica" (The transformation of the world: The method of Paulo Freire in the light of semiotics). *Interação* (São Paulo) 4(25) (Jan./Mar. 1987), pp. 17–19.

Oliveira, Admardo S. de. "Os estágios da consciência em Paulo Freire" (The stages of consciousness in Paulo Freire). *Interação* (São Paulo) 3(20) (Jun./Jul. 1986), pp. 17–20.

———. *Bibliografia comentada de/sobre Paulo Freire* (A detailed bibliography on Paulo Freire). Vitória: UFES, 1987.

Oliveira, Admardo S. de, et al. *Introdução ao pensamento filosófico* (An introduction to philosophical thinking). São Paulo: Loyola, 1985.

Oliveira, Rosiska Darcy de, and Pierre Dominicé *Freire versus Illich.* Genebra, Suiça, IDAC (document n. 8), dez. 1975 (Geneva: IDAC (document no. 8) (Dec. 1975).

Oliveira, Rosiska e Miguel Darcy de. *Guiné-Bissau: reinventar a educação* (Guiné-Bissau: Reinventing education). Lisbon: Livraria Sá Costa/IDAC, 1978.

"O profeta do be-a-bá" (The ABC prophet). *Veja* (São Paulo) 563 Jun. 20, 1979, pp. 3–6. Interview with Claudius Ceccon.

Paiva, Vanilda Pereira. *Educação popular e educação Brasileira* (Popular education and Brazilian education). São Paulo: Loyola, 1973.

———. *Paulo Freire e o nacionalismo desenvolvimentista* (Paulo Freire and developmentist nationalism). Rio de Janeiro: Civilização Brasileira, 1980.

Palácios, Jesús. *La cuestión escolar: críticas y alternativas* (The school question: critics and alternatives). Barcelona: Laia, 1984.

"Paulo Freire: a alfabetização é um ato político" (Paulo Freire: Literacy is a political act). *Cadernos do terceiro mundo* (Rio de Janeiro) 28 (Oct./Nov. 1980), pp. 34–39. Interview with Paulo Cannabarava Filho.

"Paulo Freire com a palavra" (Paulo Freire with the word). *Proposta* (FASE, Rio de Janeiro) 16 (Mar. 1981), pp. 4–10.

"Paulo Freire: eu quero ser reinventado" (Paulo Freire: I want to be reinvented). *Psicologia Atual* (São Paulo, Spagat) 3(13) (1980), pp. 14–17.

"Paulo Freire, exclusivo: quem inaugura a violência não é violentado, mas quem violenta" (Paulo Freire, exclusive: He who begins violence is not violated, but he who is violated). *Revista de cultura Vozes (Vozes Cultural Journal)*. Petrópolis, I(76) (Jan. 1982), pp. 51–60.

"Paulo Freire, no exílio, ficou mais brasileiro ainda" (Paulo Freire, in exile, became even more Brasilian). *O Pasquim*. (Rio de Janeiro) 462 (May 5, 1978), pp. 13–14. Interview with Claudius Ceccon and Miguel Paiva.

Pistrak. *Fundamentos da escola do trabalho* (Fundamentals of Work). São Paulo: Brasiliense, 1981.

Poster, Cyril, and Jürgen Zimmer, eds. *Community Education in the Third World*. London: Routledge, 1992. Preface by Paulo Freire.

Puiggrós, Adriana. "Prólogo." In Paulo Freire and Frei Betto, *Esa escuela llamada vida* (This school called life), pp. 7–63. Buenos Aires: Legasa, 1988.

Purpel, David E. *The Moral and Spiritual Crisis in Education: A Curriculum for Justice and Compassion in Education*. Granby, Mass.: Bergin & Garvey, 1989. Introduction by Paulo Freire and Henry A. Giroux.

"*Quem tem medo de Paulo Freire?*" *(Who's afraid of Paulo Freire) O Pasquim* (Rio de Janeiro) 498: (Jan. 1979), pp. 8–9, 12–18.

Reimer, Everett. "O papel revolucionário da educação" (The Revolutionary Role of Education) In *A escola está morta* (School is dead), pp. 140–59. Rio de Janeiro: Francisco Alves, 1979.

Rogers, Carl Ramson. *On Becoming a Person*. Boston: Houghton Mifflin, 1961.

_____. Rogers, Carl Ransom. *Freedom to Learn*. Columbia, Ohio: Charles E. Merril, 1969.

———. *On Personal Power*. New York: Delacorte Press, 1977.

Rother, Larry. "Radical Theorist Takes His Message to the World." *New York Times*, 19 August 1986.

Rossi, Wagner Gonçalves. *Pedagogia do trabalho: caminhos da educação socialista*. (Pedagogy of work) (Paths Toward a Socialist Education). São Paulo: Moraes, 1981.

Salem, Helena, ed. *A igreja dos oprimidos* (Church of the oppressed). São Paulo: Brasil Debates, 1981.

Santos, Paulo de Tarso. "Pedagogia do oprimido e educação do colonizador" (The pedagogy of the oppressed and colonizer education). *Educação & sociedade* (São Paulo, Cortez & Moraes) 1(3) (May 1979), pp. 24–36.

Sarup, Madan. "O solapamento das hierarquias tradicionais" (Undermining of the traditional hierarchies). In Madan Sarup, *Marxismo e educação* (Marxism and education), pp. 58–62. Rio de Janeiro: Zahar, 1980.

Schmied-Kowarzik, Wolfdietrich. "A dialética do diálogo libertador de Freire" (The dialecticism of Paulo Freire's liberating dialogue). In *Pedagogia dialética: de Aristóteles a Paulo Freire* (Dialectic pedagogy: From Aristotle to Paulo Freire), pp. 68–80. São Paulo: Brasiliense, 1983.

Shannon, Patrick. *Broken Promises: Reading Instruction in Twentieth-Century America*. Granby, Mass.: Bergin & Garvey, 1989. Introduction by Paulo Freire and Henry A. Giroux.

Shor, Ira. *Critical Teaching and Everyday Life*. Boston: Southend Press, 1980.

Skidmore, Thomas E. *Politics in Brazil: 1930–1964; an Experiment in Democracy*. Oxford: Oxford University Press, 1967.

Souza, João Francisco de. *Uma pedagogia da revolução* (A pedagogy of revolution). São Paulo: Cortez/Autores Associados, 1987.

Spring, Joel. "The Growth of Consciousness: Marx to Freire." In *A primer of libertarian education*, pp. 61–79. Montreal, Black Rose Books: 1975.

Stockfelt, Torbjörn. *La pedagoga de la vida del trabajo* (The pedagogy of the life of work). Stockholm: Stockholm University, 1991.

Stöger, Peter-Heins. *Bewubtseinspëdagogik und Eewachsenenbildung*. Frankfurt: Haag & Hershen Verlag, 1982.

Suchodolski, Bogdan. *Teoria marxista de la educación* (Marxist theory of education). Mexico: Grijabo, 1966.

Torres, Carlos Alberto. *Educación y concientización: bases antropológicas para una education liberadora* (Education and conscientization: Anthopological basis for a liberating education). Salamanca: Sigueme, 1978.

_____. *Consciência e história: a praxis educativa de Paulo Freire* (Conciousnes and history: Paulo Freire's educational practice). São Paulo: Loyola, 1979.

_____. *Diálogo com Paulo Freire* (A dialogue with Paulo Freire). São Paulo: Loyola, 1979.

_____, ed. *Leitura crítica de Paulo Freire* (A critical reading of Paulo Freire). São Paulo: Loyola, 1981.

_____. *The Politics of Nonformal Education in Latin America*. New York: Praeger, 1990.

Torres, Rosa Maria. *Educação popular: um encontro com Paulo Freire* (Popular education: A meeting with Paulo Freire). São Paulo: Loyola, 1987.

_____. *Nicarágua: revolución popular, educación popular*. Mexico City: Editorial Linea, 1986.

Tunnermann, Carlos. *Nicarágua triunfa en alfabetización. Documentos y testemonios de la Cruzada National de Alfabetizacíon* (The literacy triumph of Nicaragua: Documents and testimonies of the National Literacy Crusade).

2d ed. San José, Costa Rica: Ministerio de Educación, Departamento Ecuménico de Investigación, 1981.

Vannucchi, Aldo, ed. *Paulo Freire ao vivo* (Paulo Freire live). São Paulo: Loyola, 1983.

Wanderley, Luiz Eduardo. *Educar para transformar* (Education for transforming). Petrópoles: Vozes, 1988.

Werebe, Maria José Garcia. "A pedagogia de Paulo Freire" (Paulo Freire's Pedagogy). In *Inovação educacional no Brasil: problemas e perspectivas* (Educational innovation in Brazil: Problems and perspectives), edited by Walter E. Garcia, pp. 257–58. São Paulo: Cortez/Autores Associados, 1980. p. 257–8.

Werthein, Jorge, ed. *Educação de adultos na América Latina* (Adult education in Latin America). Campinas: Papirus, 1985.

Willianson C., Guillermo. "Paulo Freire: 1965–1969. Su paso por Chile y el Chile por que pasó" (Paulo Freire: 1965–1969. His stay in Chile and the Chile where he stayed). Santiago: La Reina, 1991, Mimeo.

Index